HOW TO BE A
LEGENDARY
TEACHER

ADAM PROCIV

BALBOA.
PRESS
A DIVISION OF HAY HOUSE

Balboa Press books may be ordered through booksellers or by contacting:

Balboa Press
A Division of Hay House
1663 Liberty Drive
Bloomington, IN 47403
www.balboapress.com.au
1 (877) 407-4847

Print information available on the last page.

ISBN: 978-1-5043-1720-7 (sc)
ISBN: 978-1-5043-1721-4 (e)

Balboa Press rev. date: 04/11/2019

CONTENTS

"The art of legendary teaching is to pretend that you are really angry when you are in fact very calm. And to then turn around and to pretend that you are very calm when you are in fact really angry."

Adam Prociv

INTRODUCTION

THE IDEA FOR the title of this book came from a list that was placed into my hands back in my very first year of teaching, "One Hundred Ways to Compliment a Child," and a buzzword that appeared at around the same time: *legend*. According to the dictionary, the literal meaning of *legend* is an old folk tale or story. But as words get changed and re-engineered over time, *legend* came to describe a person's character or feats of greatness—someone might be a *legend* on the sporting field or a *legend* in the kitchen.

The word evolved from there into describing one's exploits within these contexts. For example, his exploits in the company became *legendary* or her exploits in her field of expertise became *legendary*. So when I came across this page with "One Hundred Ways to Compliment a Child," ranging from "That's great" to "Wonderful effort," the phrase that stood out to me the most was the one that said, "You're a legend." For some reason, this resonated with me to the point that I used it in almost every teaching situation.

I even gave the title of legendary teacher to my head teacher aide, Grace. I can still recall the beaming smile that came across her face every time I (or one of the preschoolers) said it to her. She wore it like a badge of honour, and it spread like wildfire through the child care centre that we worked in.

This leads me back to memories of my own childhood and how my mother would insist on us saying how wonderful she was before asking her for something. We learnt very quickly that the bigger the request, the more lavish the compliment had to be. I can recall to this day the one that could get you almost anything. It went something like this: "Please Mummy darling, my best friend, lovely lady, star of the mountains and of the sea." It had to be accompanied by a big hug or some flowers or whatever. This became increasingly difficult in my teenage years, when the thought of hugging my parents was definitely not cool. But as I grew into a mature adult and obtained my early childhood teaching degree, I began to appreciate this method of positive reinforcement that I had been lucky enough to be exposed to.

In my first year of teaching, I asked my mother why she made us say all these things, and she said it gave her an obvious sense of appreciation—but also, it made us more appreciative of her and her role as our parent. I went back to the day care centre armed with this new vision of how the preschoolers could be encouraged (or coerced) into stating how much of a legend I was or at least would become. As teaching manners to my students has always been a huge part of my professional ethos, I began to insist that these preschoolers address me as Adam the legend. The catchphrase of "Thank you, Adam, you're a legend" began to ring throughout the child care centre, to the point where "Adam the Legend" actually became a proper noun, with a capital *L* for *Legend*.

The best part was that these preschoolers began to address each other (and pretty much anyone they encountered) in the same way. At first, this was met with some very strange looks, but with time, it created a legendary learning culture. We all talked the talk, and to our surprise, we began to walk the walk also. This was to become my very first conscious step into the world of the power of affirmations and how they could have a fantastic impact on not only my students but my whole teaching approach.

Please remember that this book is based on my own ideas and approach. You may agree with it or you may not, and either one is fine. The aim of this book is to challenge you and lead you to develop better theories about yourself and your teaching. The issues outlined here may not work for everyone, but they're intended to give you a better sense of yourself as a teacher or educator and where you want to go with your own teaching and especially your own learning. Some aspects of this book may tend to contradict each other, just as many aspects of our modern teaching lives are contradictory. And at times throughout this book I feel that I do tend to make some points more than once and repeat some themes several times. This being that many subjects within teaching and learning do blend into one another and therefore can serve in a variety of ways. Try to see past this if you will, and as the old saying goes, "Chew on the meat and spit out the bones."

CHAPTER 1

ENERGY

E NERGY IS ONE element you will need plenty of to become a legendary teacher. You will need to use it, love it, conserve it, appreciate it, and above all, understand it. In his book *The Dancing Wu Li Masters,* Gary Zukav describes energy as something "organic." He describes the organic part as alive and growing. If something is alive and growing, then it is evolving and adapting to its immediate environment. This is how I choose to view the students I teach.

The students I am responsible for need me to view them as individual masses of energy entwined with a greater energy, which is a class or a group. Their energy is open to anything I care to teach them about. This can take the form of the obvious spoken or written words but also nonverbal cues, such as body language, facial gestures, and overall personal presentation. This idea of energy may seem a bit cosmic or out there, but that's teaching for you. All the best—or at least the most memorable—teachers I have come across take this slightly offbeat approach. As we are all spiritual beings, it is only obvious that our collective energies are what go into making up our immediate reality.

As an early childhood teacher, I learned very quickly how young children respond positively to my energy and how this can dictate the course of a lesson, a small-group session, or even a teaching day. The art of good teaching is about tuning into the energy of your classroom, knowing how to manipulate that energy, and then guiding it and ultimately enhancing it.

As a teacher, your primary role is to create good energy. This can take the form of the presentation of yourself through positive body language and personal confidence. The question to ask yourself is: "Am I the teacher I would love to be taught by?" If the answer is a resounding yes, that's fantastic. But if the answer is no, then some more personal investigation needs to take place. More on that later.

Zukav also describes energy as part of our physical and spiritual vibration. He outlines this beautifully in his wonderful book *The Heart of the Soul,* where he goes into more detail about how you can align your personality with your soul in perfect vibration. Everything in the physical world has a specific vibration. As a teacher, you can relate to your energy as your own specific vibration.

Have you ever had a situation where you just clicked with someone instantly and didn't known why? Have you ever been in a situation that felt completely right for you? That's when your energy and vibration are perfectly aligned with your soul or purpose. This can be a purpose just to a specific task or to an environment, a job, or a place. The best aspect of this as a teacher is that your students' little inner radars (their vibrations) will instantly pick up on whether you are aligning yourself with that purpose.

As a teacher, I have experienced this many times. I have walked into some schools and felt completely welcome, and in others, I have felt completely distant. I have met students and had an instant rapport with them, and not so much with others. But your vibration can be altered to suit a particular situation or person if you wish.

My wonderful masseur, Helen from Cairns, told me this about six months ago. She is a former primary school teacher herself and a current yoga and meditation teacher. She told me that if I went home and found a quiet patch of grass or bare earth, I could change my vibration by jumping vigorously up and down on that spot for one minute. At first, I thought this sounded a bit out there, but I did know that Helen was a very wise woman and that she was telling me this because she cared for me enough to want me to move forward spiritually in my life. So I tried it a few times and didn't feel much different—other than being a little shaken up (literally). Then I began to notice very subtle changes in the way I saw things.

Another great sign from the heavens came a little while later, when I read a fantastic quote from Wayne Dyer's book *Inspiration* (he actually says this in several other books too): "When you change the way you look at things, then the things you look at change." This was a pivotal point of my teaching life, because as all teachers know, this profession takes up a lot of your mental and physical time. I began to see life differently. I saw my students as individuals who were on their own learning journeys just like me and were seeking their own truth for their own path just like me.

I know this may sound a bit philosophical, yet I feel this has always been my soul's calling within teaching. This is ultimately why I became a teacher in the first place. And it is the whole reason I've written this book: to encourage others to find their caring and compassionate purpose within the profession of teaching and education.

I have met a few individuals who were not suited to being teachers. When I asked them, for my own interest, why they became teachers, I was a little shocked by the answers. One was that their parents wanted them to go to university no matter what, and it was the only course they could get into. Another was that it seemed like a secure job.

At first, I was ready to write these people off as a negative influence on their students, because they essentially were in teaching as a way to pay the bills. But as the optimistic person I have grown to be, I was prepared to encourage them to either leave the teaching profession to those who really had a passion for it or to work their own energy to match their teaching journey. The results of this have been varied, and I need to stress that I don't wish to sound judgemental towards these individuals. But teaching is not a profession that you can go into half-heartedly.

It's the same when I have been working with teachers who are of mature years and ready to retire. Some of these teachers see retirement as a key to getting out of jail, and others see it as a path to a less complicated teaching journey. Sure, you will get tired of teaching at different points in your life, but the key is to know when it's time to change your path within teaching or to find a new journey into another profession. Your students will know when you have passed your use-by date as a teacher, and this will not make your journey any easier. In fact, like anything else, the more you try to just hold out to make it over that retirement line, the longer it will drag out.

The strangest thing I have ever seen—and this is happening more and more in recent years—is teachers retiring and then getting bored and returning to teaching to keep themselves interested in life. I believe that legendary teachers never retire. They just move into something that interests them at that particular stage in their teaching life. You could reduce your teaching load and go part-time or keep your finger in the pie, so to speak, with some casual work. I have even met a few teachers who have retired from full-time teaching and volunteer in schools, teaching and assisting with reading and literacy a day or two a week.

I also recall working casually at a school where I met a fantastic retired teacher who volunteered as a school grandparent. She even had this title on her name badge. Her role was to go purely wherever she was needed with reading or maths or just to talk with the students if they needed it, and they absolutely loved her for it. The best part was she proudly stated that she would never retire, because she loved being a teacher and being around kids.

Now back to the energy of the classroom. Your classroom needs to reflect your personal energy, including what you believe in, what you're passionate about, and of course, what interests you. It doesn't really matter what it is, as the main aim of this is not to brainwash your students into thinking the way you think or believing what you believe but to inspire them to find their own niches. Is your classroom inviting? Is it fascinating? Does it invite interaction or spark conversation? Can it tell a story about who is teaching there? Can it tell an equal story about who is learning there? This can be done through posters, displays, articles, or projects presented around the classroom to give the sense that your teaching is in fact alive.

When something is alive, it has the potential to move and grow in any direction it chooses. As a teacher, your role is to give that energy a positive avenue for this to thrive and to evolve even further. I recall my second-year university teaching practicum and how the teacher's classroom was in fact alive. My university supervisor commented that these students (seven-year-olds) had a myriad of visual and interactive activities awaiting them each and every day they were there.

Remember that your classroom is your domain. It is your blank canvas, your rock waiting to be sculpted. You can pretty much decorate it and display it any way you choose. Now the obvious question is, how much time can teachers spend on enhancing their physical classroom? And the answer is, as much as they want.

Forget about what other teachers think, say, or do. Yes, you will get some great ideas to enhance the energy of your classroom, but ultimately, you decide what goes into this work of art. And it is just that: a work of art. Every part of your physical classroom environment reflects your inner environment and the personal energy you bring to it. This may sound very spiritual, but that's the whole point of this book: to take the spiritual part of ourselves and project this into a positive medium for helping others, which in my case—and presumably yours—is teaching. But even if you are not a professional, at the core of our being, we are all teachers. Our sole aim in this human experience called life is to spread influence (hopefully for good) to others—to share our ideas and passions about what makes us really tick.

On the same level, we are all learners. We are spiritual beings striving to learn more about ourselves, and we are striving to understand our place in this world and universe, striving to better ourselves or at least make life better for ourselves. This energy once again comes from deep inside that part of us that makes us want to share our passion with others and ultimately get the most out of every part of our lives.

This may seem very optimistic and maybe a little naïve. In his book *Excuses Begone*, Wayne Dyer describes his approach as being seen as "Pollyanna … ish." This is the story of the young girl who always sees the positive in everything. And as Wayne describes his approach, he says that yes, it is optimistic to view life and our experiences this way, because being negative about anything won't get you anywhere. Positive energy will always attract more positive energy. There will still be plenty of negative energy out there, but you can choose not to engage it. Acknowledge it and be aware of it, but do not partake of it.

Of course, students' energy within the classroom can generate negative energy. There will be a host of social, emotional, personal, and spiritual problems in the classroom. This is inevitable, yet not overwhelming. For if you truly believe that every problem you face in your classroom has a solution, you're already halfway there. If you just want to sit on your laurels and complain and whine about the state of the nation, that's fine too. That energy will either evolve and grow or stagnate. The choice is always yours. Be the teacher you want to be and the one you are meant to be.

This may sound like some locker room pep talk, but teaching is nothing more than a game. Your game field is your classroom, and you are the head coach of your team. Your team will have good days and not-so-good days; it's how you perceive your victories and losses that will ultimately give you a sense of accomplishment and fulfilment.

In his book *Unlimited Power*, Tony Robbins describes energy as the fuel of excellence. He talks about physiology as an important part of projecting positive energy. This is one component of my teaching that breeds long-term success. Physiology pertains to the positive parts of me on the inside that gets expressed on the outside. What you see is what you get. And for the most part, it's all positive. So stand up straight, believe in yourself, and look the part. How you are perceived by your students says a lot to them about how serious you are about helping them to learn.

Be the captain of your ship and steer it wherever you want to go. Your students will pick up your energy and enthusiasm and run with it. It's not about getting everyone on board. It's not about making everyone conform. It's about giving your students the best opportunities to make informed decisions, to explore and question the world they are experiencing, to find their place in their universe, and to be part of something bigger than themselves.

As a teacher, I'm constantly asked how my day was. The best part of this is that as I have gained more experience as a teacher, I have learned that so-called "good" days can come in a myriad of ways. I've had days where everyone is on my back and nothing seems to go to plan. But then at the end of all this chaos, one student comes up, gives me a hug, and tells me how wonderful I am. I've had countless days like this.

Experience has also taught me that a so-called "bad" day is again just a matter of perception. An experience of any kind is neither good nor bad but rather just how we see it. If you are projecting good energy into your classroom and life in general, you can't help but see the positive in everything. Not that things will always go your way; quite often, it's the opposite. But if you show up each day in front of your students ready to see the best in them and their potential, magic truly can happen.

The big ask of me as a teacher, and I ask it of you also, is this: Are you the teacher you wished you had as a student? Are you fulfilling your dream of expanding and enhancing young minds and giving them the best opportunities to learn? Are you doing this for yourself as a teacher? Does your energy give off a sense that you want to be in front of a classroom or even in a school? Do your beliefs and passions come through what you speak about and act upon? Are you prepared to push boundaries or limitations in your thinking about what is so-called "good" education and what is just robot teaching?

These are all important questions that you will come across many times in your teaching career and in your life in general. For me, as a teacher, the two are very much interchangeable. They feed each other and ultimately enhance each other.

As a preschool teacher for many years, I have been asked how I ran my classroom. I responded the same way each time: by saying that I treated the students like they were in the Marine Corps. This may sound strange, but that's the value of good teaching. Good teaching sets a precedent of personal discipline on which a good foundation is built. If students—especially young children, such as toddlers and preschoolers—are taught self-discipline, this can flow into every aspect of their lives.

As a preschool teacher, I was responsible for setting a solid foundation on which my student's educational values would be built. I always saw this role in a metaphorical sense, like building a house. I would lay the slab and set the foundations which the teachers for the following grade would build upon. If these foundations were implemented correctly, the students and their creative energy would flow easily into the next level of education.

The amazing thing about your students' energy—or in most of my teaching experiences young children's energy—is that there is a never-ending supply of it. This energy comes in an abundance that never ceases to amaze me. In fact, the best part of being a preschool teacher for all those years was the way the children's energy would spur me on whilst my energy would do the same for them. It was the strangest win–win situation I have ever experienced. And the best part was that it happened for many years on a day-to-day basis.

Just yesterday, I was approached and affectionately hugged in the middle of a busy shopping centre (mall) here in Cairns by a twenty-year-old woman I taught exactly fifteen years ago as a preschooler.

The best part was (and I'm really trying hard not to cry as I type this) that this twenty-year-old began to become that five-year-old I knew all those years ago as we reminisced about the year I taught her. Now, she had the advantage that I had become good friends with her parents over the years and had seen her many times before. But just to see her grow and develop into a well-balanced and well-adjusted individual gave me some serious positive energy.

This concept is not new. I'm sure if you speak with any legendary teachers who have been around for a very long time, they will share similar stories. This to me is the essence of fantastic energy that you can share with your students both past and present.

This leads me to the idea of how energy can actually excite you and inspire you—and of course do the same for your students. I have lost track of the number of times parents have begged to have their children in my class. In many cases, I have had requests for this several years in advance. Parents come up and tell me that I can't go anywhere for the next couple of years, as their child has to be taught by me.

I did actually have the privilege of teaching two girls from separate families in a prep class many years ago and then again a few years later in a grade 4 class at a different school. The fact that I was great friends with both sets of parents made this a very memorable experience. The best part was sharing my experiences with the other grade 4 students about what these two girls were like in prep. I even treated the class to a slide show of photos that I took of them as prep students.

This was yet another example of the advantage of being a preschool/prep teacher. We were required to take photos of the students doing different assessment tasks. I would take extra photos of the students and give all these to the parents at the end of the year as a visual record of their child's first year at school. This was a lot of extra work on my part, but the heartfelt thanks I would get from these parents for such a simple thing as making their child feel special was priceless. (I am struggling not to cry as I type this too.)

Back to this self-perpetuating energy of young children: you can create it within your classroom. I have created it with older students and even with high school students. This energy has an unusual ability to jump around and get transported to other classrooms and other students.

In my time as a grade 4 teacher, I would have students from other classes come in for rotational maths and religion lessons each week. I would be subjected to a barrage of complaints about how their teacher wasn't "fun" like me—how their teacher was way too serious about teaching. I would obviously take the professional high road and explain that all teachers are different in their own way and can only work to their strengths. I would also point out that I spent many years working as a play-based preschool teacher and trained myself in making education a worthwhile learning experience through having fun. Occasionally I would just tease these children and tell them that it was too bad they weren't in my class full-time.

But even as I explore this notion of interactive energy, I can honestly state that I have never consciously set out to ever be a fun teacher. In fact, I have purposely gone out of my way to be very strict and have always seen my role as a kind of drill sergeant. This I've found over the years has enabled me to establish a clear set of expectations within which I can allow a greater sense of explorative learning to take place. When all is said and done, if I am going to try to teach someone something, I would prefer to lay down the ground rules first and then introduce the fun aspect later to keep things interesting.

Another interesting thing about energy is how it can be used in conjunction with synergy. Stephen R. Covey, in his fantastic book *The Third Alternative*, describes in great detail how synergy can be a highly effective communication tool when used correctly. He notes that the concept is highly misunderstood, especially since the business world has taken this word and misconstrued it to mean positivity in business acquisitions and takeovers. The real meaning, according to Covey, is the ability to look for possible outcomes in any given situation which have yet to be discovered. The simple notion of one plus one equals two can suddenly become one plus one equals one hundred or even a thousand. But this simple notion must be given a chance to grow and develop and to evolve into a better alternative where all parties involved feel equal and valuable and are given the opportunity to contribute to a common goal.

In education, third alternative thinking can take you as a teacher and your students to some amazing and fantastic places when, as the teacher, you step back from the traditional thinking that you are there to teach and students are there to learn. Covey even makes an interesting yet highly valid point of suggesting that you allow yourself to learn as you teach. You could take this a step further by engaging in more personal learning through being willing to share your personal expertise with you students as you actually continue to learn from them.

I know from personal experience that the more open I am to not so much what my students know but more what they can contribute to our classroom, the more innovation takes place. It's the ultimate in stepping out of the box to actually see what it is that you as a teacher can't see, and then in turn allowing your students to participate in a judgement-free environment in which all ideas and opinions are equally valued and listen to. This is a radical step in education, as it creates an environment where traditional ideas of "I'm the boss and that's it" cannot survive.

Your students still need to know that you as the teacher are responsible for your classroom culture. But this thinking gives them a certain amount of responsibility into how much of their own teaching and learning they wish to participate in. Some of my best teaching ideas have come from my students. When I have been brave enough to create an environment where students know there are no silly ideas and everyone's opinion is equal, we have had the pleasure of participating in blue-sky thinking: that is, the sky's the limit, and even the strangest ideas breed innovative and creative thought processes that can lead everyone concerned (teacher and students alike) in some truly fantastic directions.

Self-belief is at the core of this fantastic energy, and you as the teacher can produce and manipulate this energy for yourself and for your students any way you choose. Sure, you will have to follow curricula and procedures, but even within these is an energy of freedom that not many teachers can see. It's like Gary Zukav writes in *The Heart of the Soul:* "You will see it when you believe it."

Much of the energy we create as teachers comes from our own self-beliefs about how we interpret our ability to learn. A healthy level of common sense and suspicion will serve you well in making better-informed decisions. Yet this must be balanced with a healthy level of faith and calculated risk. Nothing is guaranteed from anything, and each situation will bring its own results. It's how we use these results as teachers that determines our next move.

Unfortunately, in education in general, anything different or radical in thought is not heavily encouraged or promoted. Education, as it stands presently, is more about conformity and getting the right results, mainly through academic achievement. There are, however, small pockets of different thought that are slowly expanding into such areas as prioritising educational balance with things of equal importance, such as mental health and well-being.

I can't quote exact figures on this, but I hear stories about how prescription drugs for well-being, such as Prozac, are being taken by society in ridiculous quantities. Alcohol abuse costs billions of dollars to our communities due to people not being properly educated about its causes and effects. As teachers, we keep hearing more and more about how many of our students are drugged to the eyeballs with Ritalin to ensure they are controllable. And yes, I do believe in traditional medicines and that their advancements have done fantastic things for our modern world. But as teachers, I feel it's more important to instil our students with a good sense of themselves before we try to introduce them to anything else.

This can create a fantastic energy that cannot be quashed or obliterated or destroyed, ever. Our students will be able to carry it with them like a self-knowing and self-healing tool that will serve them for life. I've seen it and I wholly believe it, and I would like to encourage you to find it for yourself in whatever way you feel comfortable. Once again, you will see it when you believe it.

As your classroom is a reflection of your own energy, it is also a reflection of your passion. And passion is what students of any age are drawn to. This is the magic elixir that can make or break a great teaching situation and allow your students to follow their own passions. For me, teaching is not about pumping your students with facts or figures but rather presenting them with opportunities to build on their own interests and energies.

This is easier said than done when there are curriculums to be followed and academic standards to be adhered to, but it's not impossible. Legendary teachers can put their own energy and spin into any topic or subject and make it interesting to their chosen audience. When politicians speak to a group of voters, they use the language of that particular group of people. Teaching with passion and enthusiasm is no different. Legendary teachers learn to walk the walk and talk the talk to accommodate many different types of ages and personalities of students.

I recall telling a junior teacher that to be successful with different types of students, one must become a bit like a chameleon and be able to slide comfortably between different teaching and social situations. This enables you to meet individuals where they're at, especially when they are your students. This can also be very beneficial when branching out and networking in other educational circles to expand your knowledge and expertise.

Another important aspect of energy in your classroom is to have plenty of it for yourself. On a purely simple and spiritual level, you as an individual have access to all the energy you will ever need through the cosmic universe. Whatever energy you believe is available to you will be, and the fantastic thing is that all you have to do is believe it. It's all just a matter of mindset.

I recall a story that my mother told me about when my sister was in labour with her first child (my nephew). The labour itself went for about seventeen hours or so through the afternoon and over the space of that entire evening. In the early hours of the next morning, my mother asked my sister to please push the baby out, as she was unbelievably tired and wished to go home. At this, my sister whined and complained about also being ridiculously tired, and she didn't think she had it in her. Nevertheless, she summoned up the energy for one final push, and hurrah! My nephew finally made his way into the world. The midwife placed my newly born nephew onto my sister's chest, and as my mother described it, she saw right before her very eyes my sister's face light up with pure energy that came from heaven itself. All the tiredness and fatigue just seemed to melt away into thin air.

I use this tale to emphasise the point that we can summon energy from places within ourselves that we didn't know we had. It's kind of like an inner strength that we all possess but only choose to use when the situation calls for it. It's like the superhuman strength that individuals can summon when placed in a position to save someone's life. There are thousands of these stories floating around about mild-mannered people lifting cars and heavy objects off people to save their lives. This energy is always available to you, and the best way to access it is just to believe you can. Get motivated into finding out more about what motivates you and how you can stay motivated, and you will be absolutely amazed at what you can achieve.

As a teacher, you will at some point become unbelievably tired—physically, mentally, and of the profession in general. When this occurs, you will need to be able to take the necessary steps to make sure that you are able to get back into the game and push on.

CHAPTER 2
THE REAL WORLD

T HE REAL WORLD of teaching is every bit as fascinating as it is scary. It's like a new beginning in every stage of your life, both as a teacher and as a spiritual being. Teaching is one profession where you can be lucky enough to share the best of yourself in so many ways whilst helping your students create their own version of success, whatever that may be. And just like every new stage of your life as a new teacher, you must prepared to start at the bottom and, over time, work your way up.

Teaching is one of those rare professions that can open up so many employment opportunities and allow you to move in so many different directions. As spiritual beings, our most important role as teachers is to allow God or the universe or whatever it is you may believe in to guide you to where you need to be as a teacher—and more importantly, to allow you to fully experience your teaching journey through the many experiences and phases it will bring. If your teaching journey is to be fully experienced, you must be open to where it will lead and be content in the knowledge that the right experience will always present itself when it's meant to.

Unfortunately, many people enter the teaching profession with a focus on getting a good job with the right kind of school. This is true for only part of your teaching journey. When you allow yourself to just *be*, the best learning situation will find you.

When I was a new graduate with an early childhood teaching degree, I was told that being a male and one with an enthusiastic disposition, I would be snapped up. Well, in the real world, nothing could have been further from the truth. I recall going down to the quick copy office and copying my CV a staggering forty times. After several months of this, the quick copy manager was so taken by my dedication and my patience that he was almost going to give me a job out of sympathy.

Out of those forty applications I sent away, do you want to guess how may interviews I was invited to? Only two. One day care centre offered me an interview just because they had never heard of a male graduate with an early childhood teaching degree. Another day care centre was a little more enthusiastic about moving forward with the times and saw me as an opportunity to perhaps experiment with having a male preschool teacher. They actually already had a male teacher's aide, so they were halfway there at least.

The first interview was a bit like a medical examination. They mentally poked me and prodded me to see if I was all there and didn't have any significant flaws as a male or as a new graduate. I kind of got the impression that they were never going to be so brave as to risk employing me for what their clientele might think of me. I didn't really feel that treating me like a suspected paedophile was going to make me more agreeable to their establishment.

The second interview went slightly better, but I got that sinking feeling all new graduates do when they know they are competing with a lot of people for only a handful of jobs. At least this second day care centre was run by a Christian organisation, and I did play the "every child needs more father figures in their life" card. I am happy to announce that God as I know Her (and yes my God is a her) did guide me to the right job, which came from this second interview. This set a real precedent in my life for how my faith and trust in the truly divine was to unfold.

In between this period of interviews and copying and sending out my CV, I had somehow acquired a casual teaching position at yet another day care centre. I had replaced the previous preschool teacher, who'd had a nervous breakdown. When I first met the staff and the children, I could clearly see why. But like I said, I went with the divine and dived headfirst into this as my introduction to preschool teaching: Hard Knocks 101.

After about three months, I could see that my life on welfare payments would at least keep me a little bit more sane in the short term. I recall coming home, collapsing onto my bed, and bursting into tears, wondering if all my time at university was worth this terrible experience. I can still hear my mother's voice in my ear saying that it couldn't be that bad, and could I just stick it out to see whether it would either improve or perhaps something better would come up. I secretly wanted the job at the Christian day care centre for which I'd had the interview a month or so previously, but at this point, I was quite happy to just go back on welfare.

I prayed to God to show me a sign, and after a very restless night of tossing and turning, She did. At six the next morning, I received a call from the Christian centre supervisor offering me the job. They asked when I could start, and I almost said at nine o'clock that very morning, but I played the noble card and said I would have to stick it out for at least another week at this other centre as a gesture of my good will.

It's amazing how you can put up with almost anything when you can see the finish line. I recall going back to the day care centre that morning and announcing to the office manager that I had been offered another permanent job. She asked if I would like to put it on a sandwich board to let all the kids and parents know. I asked her for some suggestions, and to my surprise, she laughed and said, "How about something like 'Yippee, I'm outta here!'" It turned out that she didn't really like being there either, and in some strange way, in that moment, we became kindred spirits of seeking better things in life.

So I left that centre and embarked on yet another phase of my teaching journey. As I reflect back on this experience all these years later, I know that divine guidance was carrying me through what I needed to experience and more importantly, what valuable lessons I needed to learn. Unfortunately, at university, they can only teach you so much about how it is you can teach. It's a small snippet of what's to come. It's an introduction on a grand scale, but the real test comes when you are thrown into a classroom of your own.

Of course, there are many different types of classroom and many different types of teaching, but the message is universally the same. You are there to help others learn aspects of subjects they do not fully comprehend and enable them (whether children or adults) to understand themselves better. Competent teachers do breed competent learners, but this is only a small part of the story. The *competent* part for me comes from teaching students to fully believe in themselves and build self-confidence for themselves first. It's like the old saying: "You can't give away what you don't have." Self-love and self-confidence are things you must acquire before you can share them with others.

If there is one epidemic that we need to eradicate from our society, it is the lack of true self-belief. Sure, there are plenty of people floating around who rise to be captains of industry and pillars of society on their own. But one thing I have found in my teaching life by experience is that we all harbour many little silly insecurities. If young children are not taught to believe in themselves, they can grow into very insecure adults. Or even more importantly, into adults who hide their insecurities very well and pretend that they don't exist, using projection, machoism, bravado, anger, frustration, and a host of other negative emotions that can last a lifetime.

My eyes were really opened when I read *Your Erroneous Zones* by the wonderful and immortal Dr. Wayne Dyer. Reading this book about human behaviour gave me one of the best insights into my own limitations and how I as a teacher project these into my own world. Any great teacher or role models worth their salt need to get a copy of this book. Read it, study it, and learn to understand it. And as you do you will see first-hand everything from this book not only in your own life but in the lives of those you teach.

Another big part of your real-world learning as a teacher is to develop a healthy sense of making mistakes and self-forgiveness. We as teachers, and of course people, have somehow trained ourselves to fear our mistakes. Our society has made us self-aware through not making mistakes and seeing this as pure incompetence. I guess a better way of putting this is trying to "keep up with the Joneses" and making yourself look good to others. We want to be seen as having it all together, which in teaching as much as in life is complete nonsense. You are going to make mistakes, and you are going to learn from them. The best course of action that has served me well in my life is to see mistakes as your greatest teachers.

It's like when you were a baby, and you were learning to walk. You didn't even think about how many times you fell over; you just kept going. Unfortunately, as adults (and teachers), we like to think that we are older and therefore wiser and don't need this silly mindset anymore. Well, I can tell you, this is yet another reason why I love being a teacher and especially love working with young children, because I see that "never say die" attitude every day of my working life. I see my young students working to become better readers or spellers or better at maths or whatever and conquering their fears. This helps me immensely to remember this for myself and how important my job is to facilitate an encouraging environment which promotes mistakes as part of daily risk.

I try to construct a support framework within the classroom that values the taking of risks at the expense of feeling inadequate. I let my students know through words and actions that no-one will laugh or bully them for being different. No-one will exclude them for having different ideas or interests. Even though this sounds all very nice and a little bit airy-fairy, it actually works. I have led classrooms where students have discovered all kinds of talents and ideas within themselves purely based on a supportive climate of open learning.

Of course, this can't be applied to every subject in every situation, but it can be undertaken as an overall state of thinking, which as a teacher you can control and promote any way you want. Believe it can happen, and it will happen. Be the teacher who can actively take risks with your teaching and learning and encourage your students to do the same. You'll be amazed with the results.

I would like to further reinforce this with a personal story about how I conducted my grade 4 classes. I would first introduce a unit of work and ask the students what they knew about it already. Everyone in the class knew that there were no silly answers. No-one was ever going to laugh at them or ridicule them.

The next step would be to ask them what they themselves wanted to know about this subject. Did it interest them or not? Most students gave the standard answer of "I ddddd ... no," which in plain English means "I don't know" or could on a deeper level mean "I'm not sure of what the answer is, but with your encouragement, I will gain a greater sense of myself and therefore a greater sense of what it is I want to become more informed about." Not exactly a simple process, but once you get through the usual student boredom or bravado, you can arrive at a truly magical place of learning.

An interesting thing about this whole approach to teaching and learning is that we rarely as teachers ask our students what it is they think about something. We tend to have a society or culture that dictates a lot about how life is rather than how life can be. This comes about as a teacher when you are handed your curriculum and politely instructed to "do it or else."

Strangely enough, this does have its place in the scheme of things to ensure that educational chaos doesn't reign. But on a deeper level, it trains us to stay in line and follow the educational status quo. The old saying of "this is how we do things around here" seems to echo through every classroom and school across the land. This does give us a stable grounding to work from, but it needs to be accompanied by a greater sense of scrutiny. Firstly from teachers, then from the students themselves in a supportive environment.

The great language teacher Michel Thomas proclaimed in his teachings that you will only really retain what it is you want to know. His teaching of language was based on a need-to-know basis and therefore led his students to move into a mindset built on interest rather than obligation. As a classroom teacher, your primary role is to promote independent thought through a set curriculum. How you do this on a day-to-day basis is up to you. It becomes a test of your own creativity, and once you tap into it, it will serve you well. One tool that can help you immensely is personal reflection and meditation.

As a teacher, personal reflection is one of the most useful tools you could ever use. It can be done casually or as in-depth as you wish to go. There are limits to this, however, as you can become self-obsessed with every little incident or detail of a lesson or whatever. With experience, you can learn how to discern what is worth worrying about and what is not.

This leads me to the subject of fear within your teaching. Yes, it does exist, and yes, it can make or break you as a teacher. The first thing I suggest you do is forget about how the media portrays teachers and the education industry as a whole. Good news and good-will stories about anything to do with this are few and far between. As a general rule, every time I watch the news on TV, I am bombarded with stories about how our children can't read properly when they leave school or how our nation's test scores are way down the list of developed countries. I do myself a huge favour and completely ignore this rubbish, and also stopped watching the TV news too.

I can assure you that teachers are not to blame for any of this. In fact, I will take the moral high ground and say that no-one is to blame for these things. Yes, our education system is far from perfect, but teachers themselves do not have control over a host of circumstances they face each day in their classrooms. This can range from students having difficult home lives to there being inadequate funding for resources within the classroom. It never ceases to amaze me how our political leaders are quick to lay the blame everywhere except on themselves.

And by this, I don't wish to be passing the blame back to them, but each year in education, I see money that could improve students' lives in so many ways being allocated to big business or to projects that don't have the greater community's well-being in mind. It would be a bit like expecting a garden to grow with inadequate watering and fertilizing, and then being mystified as to why this garden is not growing properly.

Reflection is one tool you can use to get a better scope on what it is you are teaching but also how you fit into the scheme of things, both as a teacher and as a person on your own journey. Most new teachers are fairly young when entering the teaching profession. Of course, this trend has changed a lot in the past few years, with many mature graduates also making the leap. I say *leap* here, because that's exactly what teaching is: a leap of faith in the most extreme way. Sure, there are countless other noble professions that require courage, giving, and self-discipline, but teaching is in a world of its own. This world is primarily built on trust: trust that you can do what it is you are assigned to do but to also take care of the students that you teach.

As a young preschool teacher, I learnt very quickly that the trust placed upon me by the institution was huge. Yet the trust placed upon me by the parents whose children I was teaching was even bigger. As I slowly moved into primary school over many years and subsequently became friends with teachers from high school right up to university lecturers, I realised that this feeling never diminishes. It only became a bit sophisticated or in some cases a little bit more complicated. Educating your students, as I've stated before, is only part of the role you will play. Another huge component to teaching, especially in the younger years, is educating the parents and the greater community in general.

Many teachers may be scoffing and thinking to themselves that this is not possible; it's just some crazy pipe dream. But including your students' parents in their education is essential. Educating both parties is the only way to help them understand their education but also each other. This does get a lot more difficult when students move into high school and the parent involvement tends to drop off somewhat. But when this happens, that is your cue as a teacher, educator, and leader to really step up and promote a culture of being involved. As much as a lot of high school students wouldn't be that encouraging of having their parents get involved with their education (or anything else in their lives for that matter), it is a key time to get to know your students through their parents and their home life to help promote better understanding for all parties involved.

Back to the leap of faith: beginning teachers will always require something to give them that edge to succeed, and that is courage. They need courage to step out of themselves and do something they know very little or even nothing about. But that's only a small part of the story. Courage also enables you as a teacher to keep renewing or re-inventing yourself.

It took me many years of asking the right questions to get the right answers. As a new teacher especially, you need to be open to asking the right questions, even more so for new teachers of mature age. You may have some life experience behind you, and that's great, but remember that you are a beginner like everyone else and must start your new life as a teacher not so much from the bottom but from a beginner's perspective.

There are a lot of mature beginning teachers with an attitude of not wanting to ask proper questions about the essentials of teaching to gain further insight. This is not a good place to start. Use your first years as a time to observe, reflect, and do your apprenticeship. Without this aspect of cutting your teeth, you may lose out on valuable information that can be passed down from experienced teachers who have many years on the job. As for you young graduates, please also take note of this. You are at the bottom of the pile and need to work your way up. But you are in a fantastic profession that values and nurtures your creative teaching style if you are open to learning from those around you.

When all is said and done, everybody knows that teachers are there to do their best given their resources and energy levels at any given time. For those experienced teachers out there who happen to be reading this book to gain greater insight into improving their teaching, please remember to ask new teachers questions about their approach also. The learning goes both ways, and the beauty of having new teachers enter the profession at any age is that they bring a fresh set of eyes to things. I have lost count of how many new teachers have inspired me with their optimism and positive energy. That's how teachers can keep their perspective and give all students a good sense of balance with the knowledge available to them.

As far as classroom or student results go, good academic scores do not dictate who is a good teacher and who is not. I have seen many special needs teachers (and I'm always in awe of them) get success from teaching students how to write their name or even engage in a conversation. Yet our world has become results-driven. I'm not saying we should not applaud the "A" students, yet they represent a very small percentage of the students any teacher will ever teach. So the question is, what do we do with the rest? Sure, we want to enable them to bring out their best academically and to excel at whatever it is they aim for. But what about social skills and aptitude? Some of the most successful people in the world have never completed their formal schooling.

Now, I'm not advocating that we should encourage students to just settle for something academic or even to give up and drop out. Once again, this comes down to a question of belief in our students and their confidence in themselves. Success is all relative. It comes in many different forms of achievement, and as teachers, we should become more aware of all of these possibilities for our students. Sometimes in life, we aim for a goal and don't actually get there, but then we realise all the invaluable learning and growing we did along the way. Teaching is just like anything else in life: it's a journey, not a destination. Enjoy the journey and remember that everything good, bad, or indifferent has value for you the teacher and your students.

In the real world of teaching, you will be constantly confronted with conflicting views about the right way and wrong way to teach. You will be torn between what your head is telling you and what you really believe in your heart is the best way to go. I would like to emphasise this point with the great Native American Sioux saying: "The longest journey you will ever make in your life is from your head to your heart." Ultimately, this is the journey that will bring you the most inner conflict as a teacher. What you believe to be true for you as an individual and what the general belief is for a collective in teaching can be and at times will be very different.

I have known a few teachers who take pride in being different, and that's okay, but you will ride at times a very fine line when you begin to show opposition to your administration, especially when you know that your job could be at stake. You will need to discern between what's really worth getting passionate about and what isn't. The odds of getting fired as a teacher are a lot less than in most other jobs, and this is particularly true for most caring industries. This could be mainly to do with the fact that teaching doesn't produce the same types of products that a normal business or service organisation might produce. Since you are dealing with people (as in students) for clients, there seems to be a little bit more leniency with how things are done. Many policies and procedures are open to interpretation based on the fact that there could be many variables going on in each individual situation.

Even with this in mind, always be aware of how much you wish to toe the line with a situation or student or school and how much you don't. This is a very important aspect of teaching to be aware of. It will heavily dictate whether or not you will feel comfortable and content with where you are teaching and whether or not you are getting a good balance between being challenged and being bored or not feeling that your heart is really in it. Striving to become more aware of how you feel about every part of your teaching will enable you to keep following your true teaching path and allow you to get the maximum amount of satisfaction out of your working life as a teacher in the long term.

Yet another very real aspect of teaching that you will encounter is discrimination. For all the progress we think we've made over the years with gender equality, discrimination still exists. It's still very real in our modern world of teaching and in many other professions too. I'm not going to harp on about it here, but it has been one thing in my teaching that has really irritated me and brought me many experiences that were anything but pleasant.

When I first became an early childhood teacher, I went to an educator's union conference. I was the only male out of about two hundred to three hundred people attending. A greater proportion of the people attending were older women of my mother's age—the baby boomers post–World War II generation. Out of all of the people attending, I was surprised to find that only two women were actually interested in interacting with me, and one of them was an old friend from my church who I hadn't seen in a couple of years.

At one point in the conference, I could actually feel a lot of what I perceived to be hostility towards my position as a male preschool teacher. Perhaps this was just my perception at the time, but as I have always regarded myself as a highly intuitive individual, I definitely did not feel welcome there. And now that I think about it, I do recall telling the friend I saw there at that time, and she agreed with me. In fact, she said that in her experience, the early childhood industry very much needed more males to be entering this profession.

As much as I do not want to focus too much on the negatives of anything about teaching in this book, I have encountered over the years many women who felt that my mere presence in a room full of young children (or any children) was highly inappropriate. It was almost like I had to apologise for being a male. I don't mean to sound sexist when I say this, but I have felt this as a male teacher many times. I feel that some women can be sly when it comes to showing outright disapproval of a male preschool teacher. Especially when he is tall, athletic, and outgoing like me. This has led me into some very strange situations where I felt that I was always being "watched". This notion unfortunately has scared many other males from wanting to enter the early childhood profession and teaching in general.

To counter this with a more positive tone, I will share a couple of other experiences about how males (as in the dads of the preschoolers) have dealt with my presence as a male preschool teacher. I can recall very vividly the first day I started as a male preschool teacher in my first permanent teaching role. It actually took a month for the admin to decide whether or not the clientele of the child care centre were even ready for a male preschool teacher. The dads all stood at the back of the room with their arms folded giving me the death stare, like I was some kind of paedophile. This did at the time unnerve me quite a bit. This was the same greeting I was to receive from all the new dads each year as I progressed into my life as a preschool teacher.

After about the fifth year or so, I didn't care about these stares anymore, and I would even take the approach of walking up to all the new dads (much to their surprise and discomfort) and introducing myself, giving them a very firm manly handshake, and looking them square in the eye. After about a month or so, they would come in one by one to the preschool and confess that they did in fact think I was some kind of weirdo and that they now knew that I was a genuine and dedicated preschool teacher and that I was all that their kids ever talked about at home. As God is my witness, this happened so many times each year that it almost became a routine. The best part of this was that some of those dads have become my lifelong friends and almost an extension of my family, or more like I became an extension of theirs.

The strangest thing about this experience was that as much as many women have agreed that many if not all children need strong, competent, and loving men in their lives, there still seems to be an air of suspicion that every new male they meet could be some kind of sexual predator. Yet the one thing I would explain to all new parents—as a preschool and later a primary school teacher—is that with all the screening and criminal checks and paranoia around that, these measures, as imperfect as they are, are an effective deterrent.

These are my experiences with discrimination in teaching. I know that many women have faced much greater challenges when making their way in the (supposedly) male-dominated worlds of politics, the military, business, and, of course, teaching also. In the words of the great tennis player Pete Sampras, "I don't try to justify my playing to anyone, I just let my racquet do the talking." This is what I now do too. I just let my metaphorical teaching racquet do my talking for me in the classroom.

In the real world of teaching, there is one quality that a legendary teacher already possesses or can learn to achieve through diligent practice: the killer instinct. By this, I mean that as a teacher who can roll with the punches and still come out on top, you will need to develop a tough skin, especially with your students. By *toughness*, I mean that all you really need to do is stand by your convictions as a teacher. Know within yourself what you will stand for and what you won't, and make this very clear to your students through your expectations of them. They will try to take advantages in almost every situation, and you must have your game face on 24/7 to combat this. It will be the ultimate test of your survival as a teacher.

This instinct does not pertain to whether you are male or female, tall or short, heavyset or slightly built. I have seen it shine through in many different ways with many different types of teachers, but you will have to set very specific expectations with your students about how respect is given and received and then stick to it. Stand your ground, and do not be intimidated by any student or parent or even another staff member.

Sure, in some ways, this may seem a little contradictory to other parts of this book, but when you really stand by what you believe in and let this show through your teaching and that you won't compromise on certain things, you will gain the respect and recognition of all stakeholders in your teaching life. It's like the old saying, "Say what you mean and mean what you say." When your students know that you take this very seriously, it will set the right tone for everyone involved to know exactly what is expected of them.

One of the best books I have ever had the privilege of coming across was Elizabeth C. Vinton's *How to Set Limits*. This book beautifully outlines and defines how to set appropriate boundaries for children of all ages, including teenagers. I read this book like the Bible in my first few years of teaching. This I feel is yet another key to being a legendary teacher, because it defines who you are and how your role as a teacher is important to your students.

If you are teaching young children, their inner guidance radar will detect the faker or the maker within you about three seconds after they walk into your classroom. Be the king or queen of your teaching castle and let the students know who's boss. Not that you want blind obedience—you don't. But you will need to set clear parameters of what your inner beliefs are about yourself as a teacher to your students, and also how this flows into your immediate teaching environment.

One of the more recent aspects of the real teaching world that I have had the privilege of learning (slight use of sarcasm here) is that when you are consulted to speak your mind to the admin, just plainly lie. I know that this is a big call, and as teachers we pride ourselves on being honest, caring, and moral people. But I have learnt that on the very rare occasion you are ever asked if you feel that a situation at school is good, bad, or indifferent, just give a very plain business-like answer that is vague and leads to nothing.

I have spoken my mind on many occasions to various admins over the years in my teaching. Unfortunately most of these opinions that I was asked to convey or felt the need to state about something were either plainly ignored or led to me being chastised (in some cases heavily). This may paint a very bleak picture to any aspiring teacher who likes to express an opinion on certain matters. I have gone into battle many times, mostly to do with budgeting and workplace practice issues, and the total sum of my opinion and professional judgement seems to amount to, well, not much. But on a positive note I have always felt that even if as a teacher I did get ignored by the powers that be, at least I said what I believed. Ironically they sometimes came back to me many years later and stated that I was actually justified in what I said. Yes, vilification in teaching is a very strange beast.

This has at times has left me feeling very discouraged, and I have had many heated conversations with myself over the years about whether or not I wanted to continue being a teacher because of this. The one thing I have never done, to my credit, is threaten to leave a school or institution. If you do wish to do this, the administration couldn't care less if you do or not.

Now again, although I am a positive person, I have to take a slight turn for the worse on this issue and tell you that in my experience, most school and educational establishments do not care about your well-being. Sure, they will on the surface provide you with sick leave, maternity leave, counselling and just about any other kind of support you could ever want, but rest assured that the moment you're gone, you are pretty much forgotten. In this great country of Australia (or any first world nation), the governments— both state and federal—aren't really out there promoting your well-being either. When all is said and done, you are just a number to the powers that be. Sure they will love to tick a few wellbeing boxes, but that's about it.

In some rare cases, I have been able to negotiate certain conditions of my job description to suit myself or to at least improve my sense of well-being as a teacher. But these opportunities are few and far between. How do you survive this kind of thing for yourself? Learn to carve out your own little niche of sanity within the boundaries of your job role and make it work for you. You could join the union and take a stand on certain issues. I would advocate that being in a teachers union is a very positive thing, and many aspects of teachers' conditions, such as pay scales, have improved greatly as a result of this. But please be aware that when you stick your head up above the crowd and speak up about anything deemed by your admin as unpopular, you will make yourself a very big target.

Whilst we are on this subject, it's important to remember that you are on your own with your thoughts about what teaching and education mean to you. Sure, you may be able to relate well to your teaching colleagues' outlooks or be in a situation where everyone is on the same page, but essentially you will not agree with every aspect of the teaching going on around you. You may also find yourself in conflict with the expectations put on you by the powers that be, whether your admin or the district educational office or whoever. The sad thing about this is that those in charge will not always have your back. In the real world that is teaching, they will support you in many things but not everything. Be prepared to be proverbially "hung out to dry" during your teaching life a few times. But to swing this back to the positive once again, this will help you learn some fantastic life lessons.

When it comes to disputes with parents, the admin will generally side with the parents. Obviously this is just my view on this and my stated experiences, but they are once again your proverbial clients. This is not necessarily a bad thing as you learn to navigate the world that is teaching, but it is a pitfall to be aware of. If you feel at any point that you are not supported on a major issue, by all means, stand up for yourself. Gather together some evidence to support your case and make a point of it with your admin. Get the union involved if need be, but just be aware of what you are willing to follow through with and what you aren't. It's not that I want you or anybody else to be paranoid in your day-to-day teaching life. Just be aware of certain things that will appear on your teaching radar somewhere along the way. And like anything in your teaching life (and life in general), I believe these things are throw into your path to test your worth. Roll with the punches and learn to become unbelievably resilient.

In the real world, you as a teacher will find yourself feeling like a very small fish in a very big pond. This is not necessarily a bad thing, but one needs to keep in perspective how much influence you will have within your day-to-day teaching. Experience has taught me that as much as there will be times when you will want to take on the world and tell them all how misguided they are, the best thing to do is to identify how far your own sphere of influence extends and then know where your personal boundaries are set. This in the long term will help you immensely in choosing your battles and really knowing what is worth becoming passionate about and what is not. It will help you to feel balanced in your own little circle and not feel like the weight of the world is on your shoulders.

You will meet some teachers who will lead everything and be driven and seem to have connections everywhere. But that is their path and their path alone. If you see another teacher doing something you admire and you feel good about pursuing something similar, then go for it. Some people are driven by the need to be seen; they feel good about being in the political spotlight waving the banner for education. Others don't. Find what it is that you feel you personally can really make progress with and move towards that.

It's interesting to note that some (if not a lot) of my best and most fulfilling teaching moments were very simple things, like helping a preschooler learn how to skip or catch a ball, or helping an older child gain more confidence through public speaking. These for me are the memorable moments that have really made a huge difference to my little sphere of influence. Ultimately, the message here is that when you feel good about what you can control in your teaching and what you know you can't, this gives you a better perspective about what changes you can make to your approach and to your day-to-day teaching practice overall.

To add one more point, the real world of teaching is that a lot of what you will be instructed to teach will come from your superiors. The harsh reality of teaching, just like any other bureaucratic system, is that the people at the top who make the rules generally have very little idea about what's really going on down on the ground. You will be faced with some very good things worth teaching, for the most part, but then you will also be presented with some absolute rubbish. As you determine where your sphere of influence will reach, do what St. Francis of Assisi famously suggested: "Do what's necessary then do what's possible and then suddenly you'll be doing the impossible."

When I was moved into teaching grade 4 after spending nearly my whole teaching life with preschoolers, I found that the curriculum for these students had been written by high school teachers—or at least someone who had no idea about what a grade 4 student should be learning. This caused me a lot of angst, as I knew that these students were being set up to fail. After a few years of this, my sphere of influence no longer had any bearing on this grade level, so I requested a change. The unfortunate thing is that the current grade 4 teachers in this same school are still just as stressed out as I was a few years back. At some point, I think either the admin or even the bureaucracy might wake up to the fact that they can't actually retain a lot of teachers in this defunct system. Either that, or they will be happy to use new graduate teachers as cannon fodder for their own political interests. We'll see.

CHAPTER 3

THE JOURNEY

THE MOST IMPORTANT thing to remember as you embark on your teaching journey is that you should be in it for the long haul. In this day and age of modern technology, where instant gratification is the norm, most people expect to get instant results for things that take years to perfect. And teaching is no different. Becoming a legendary teacher will not just happen overnight. That would be like saying you could pick up a tennis racquet for the first time one day and then be ready to play at Wimbledon the next. It takes years of hard work, dedication, and practice to develop and refine your skills. The best part is that if you take on the right mindset, you can learn the most unbelievable things along the way.

If you are a beginning teacher, once again I urge you to learn from those around you as much as you can. Get yourself a small notepad and write down all your good ideas. Then take these and make of them what you will. If you are a new teacher of mature age with some life experience behind you, again please do not assume that you know it all. Even if you have experience with education through being a parent, being the teacher in the classroom is a very different ball game.

Make a conscious effort to share ideas with you colleagues and teaching associates. Do not try to be a know-it-all or burn yourself out to impress anyone else, as it doesn't work. All you will end up doing is alienating yourself from the very support network you will need to rely on to keep you going. Be smart and keep an open mind. And always remember that as a teacher, you are part of a team, and you are always on the same team.

There is no such thing as healthy competition between teachers over anything, and there is also no such thing as a friendly rivalry. Respect each of your teaching colleagues' differences and teaching approaches, and respect your students' differences also in the same manner. We are all not here to experience the same thing on our teaching journey, nor do we all want to operate like a bunch of robots pushing out students on some educational conveyor belt. Be yourself and respect others' individuality also.

As much as schools and various organisations may set a certain standard for different types of teaching, you should be essentially seeking your own path for your own teaching experiences. This is a very strange paradox. As much as we wish to treat all of our students equally, in reality we can't. As much as we wish to allow them to find their own learning path, they still have to follow certain rules of conformity. With teaching, the paradox is even more evident. You will need to follow expectations or protocols of the institution within which you teach to keep your job but also to set a certain standard of academic achievement.

You will begin to find that the way to successfully teach your students is to adapt the curriculum to the immediate environment which your students can relate to. There are as many ways to do this as there are teachers in the world. Rely on your teaching experiences to give you the confidence you need to explore new avenues of thought in regards to the curriculum and how you can deliver it successfully to your students. The trick is to be again in a constant state of reflection and critical thinking about what you are teaching and how your students' needs fit into this. This reflection can be a daily habit, or it can take place weekly or whenever it suits you.

The most difficult part of this is to be able to keep this reflection and critical thinking in balance with everything else. It is very easy to begin to overanalyse every part of your teaching (especially if you are a beginner) and become obsessed with delivering perfect lessons. The fact is that whether you are a beginning teacher or a senior teacher, you are still going to make a lot of mistakes. The saving grace for you in this arena is that if you are not making mistakes, then you are not trying.

Not that you want to just stumble from one blunder to the next, but keep a healthy attitude and outlook, especially towards new things and elements of your teaching that take time to perfect. Have fun with this and remember to be your own biggest fan. Balance all of this with little rewards and compliments to yourself. Give yourself positive and constructive pep talks about what you are doing well and what needs more attention. And always believe in yourself and your abilities.

The teaching game is all a process of hit and miss, trial and error. Sometimes there are more misses than hits, and definitely, in the beginning, lots of errors and trials. Some lucky souls will have a natural flare for this profession, and others won't. But just like anything in life, success doesn't necessarily come to those with the most talent but to those who have sheer determination and the will to be a legendary teacher.

On your teaching journey, you will go through many different phases and incarnations of yourself. The one thing I cannot stress enough is not to become complacent with a situation because it feels secure or even comfortable. I have been there many times in my teaching life, and I have found that the more diversity I have encountered with different teaching situations, the more I have grown and developed as a teacher. So as a new teacher, please do not necessarily strive to teach at a "good" school. Once again develop a genuine trust that God, The universe or your teaching angels (or whatever it is that you believe in) will guide you to the right situation for you.

And yes, I use the words *angels* very seriously, because at some point you will begin to realise that there is always a power greater than yourself guiding you along your teaching journey. There may be some readers out there thinking that this is all New Age fluff, but the one thing I have learned on my teaching journey is that divine guidance is one of the most powerful sources you can tap into. There will be other teachers or colleagues who won't subscribe to this notion. There will even be some who will ridicule your beliefs. But I challenge those critics to look within themselves and really get to know themselves first.

When one takes the huge step of beginning a new journey, such as teaching, one must develop a certain set of new skills. How well you can implement those skills depends on your own self-belief. This comes from the ability to know yourself and know that you are just one part of the vast universe we all live in. Tapping into yourself can open the doors to a whole new world of possibility and learning.

As you embark on this journey called teaching, you are going to encounter many weird and wonderful situations around what it is that you will actually have to teach. These come in the form of curricula. Your primary job is to teach the prescribed curriculum, which is a no-brainer, as that's what you are paid to do. But to develop into a good teacher—or may I say great or even a legendary teacher—one needs to go outside the square somewhat. Yes, this will bring discomfort; yes, it will bring conflict. But without these important aspects of your teaching life, you will not be able to let your passion flow.

My passion is flowing right now as I write this book. I very much expect that what I write about in these pages will bring resistance and even conflict to these ideas and concepts; to that, I say great. I have no fear of what other teachers or other people in general think of my teaching approach. We are all different with different ideas, beliefs, likes, and dislikes. In teaching, as in life, we do not all need to follow the same drumbeat. Yes, you must follow your job description and your ethical code of conduct, but with the approach that this is yours and yours alone. Develop it, enhance it, nurture it. Allow it to have a life of its own.

You will undoubtedly find yourself faced with situations where you don't agree with what it is you are required to teach. The longer you teach, the more you will find these situations occurring. Unfortunately, this can have a negative effect on your approach and how you view teaching. The key here is to never give up your passion for what you believe in.

History is littered with people who had a burning desire to share their knowledge with others even at great personal cost. Now, obviously, teaching is a paying job like any other, and it makes good sense not to do certain things if you know they could get you fired. But at the same time, how deeply does your passion run? The beauty of teaching is that if you do not find yourself in a cohesive situation within which you can strive, then look for other avenues of employment. Do not be arrogant about it and make demands and then cause a fuss and storm out. Instead, see it like just another phase in your teaching journey, something placed in your path to enable you to experience it.

See it, hear it, feel it, and then use it as a springboard to something new, something different. Are you open to the possibility of what you're not seeing in a situation? Are you missing some crucial element that could enable you to make a better decision about things? I encourage you to enhance and develop this openness to your teaching approach and to your life in general.

Remember that some aspects of teaching cannot be learned all at once. What you learn in your first year will be very different from what you learn in your second. Even though you will gain competence in the chosen field within which you wish to teach, things will always need a little shake-up from time to time. Be brave, be bold, and change fields every couple of years. Change schools or teaching levels or whatever you open yourself up to.

Nothing makes me sadder than to hear of teachers who are in the same job year in and year out. It's predictable, it's comfortable, but it serves no purpose for you as a higher learner yourself. As Tony Robbins put it in his book *Awaken the Giant Within*, whatever is not growing and evolving dies. Do you want to be spiritually dead? Do you want to just flounder because you're too scared of what's out there? Once again, learn whatever you can from every situation and take that knowledge and use it to your advantage. Robbins wrote, "Knowledge in itself is not power. It's how you use that knowledge that creates true power." See every teaching situation as an opportunity to gain knowledge and also an understanding of how to use that knowledge.

Now even as you read this, you may be thinking, *Wait a minute. This is not as easy as it sounds. I'm teaching in a less than ideal school, or I'm still getting my head around a new curriculum, and it's just not that simple.* I agree, it's not that easy to adjust and adapt to any new situation or information. As the great Scottish motor-racing champion Jackie Stewart said in a television interview, "Nothing in my life that has ever come easily has ever been any good."

Change is always difficult in the beginning. But the concept of perception and personal belief is always easy. Dr. Wayne Dyer explains this beautifully in his book *Your Erroneous Zones*. He describes in great detail the notion of how one's thoughts can lead to self-fulfilling beliefs, and in this context it's related to addiction. He shows how the thought processes behind decisions are actually quite simple.

I would like to take this opportunity to share a story about my late grandpa and his change in perception regarding smoking. Anyone who has ever tried to quit smoking will know how difficult this is to do, as nicotine is one of the most addictive substances on earth. He was at a New Year's Eve party back in 1985. He was rolling a cigarette and was asked by a friend why he did that. He replied by saying that it was cheaper; he had done it for so many years, it just seemed like the sensible thing to do.

The friend then asked him how long he had actually smoked. My grandpa thought about this for a minute and then said, "Fifty years. I began smoking when I was fourteen, and I'm now sixty-four, so yes, it's been fifty years."

The friend then asked my grandpa, half in jest, if he had ever thought about giving up.

"No," my grandpa replied.

"What would it take for you to give it up?" the friend asked.

"I don't know," my grandpa replied. "Perhaps an act of God."

"I bet you can't give it up right now," the friend offered.

My grandpa thought for a moment and then looked from the unlit cigarette in his hand back to his friend. He declared this was to be the last cigarette he was ever going to smoke.

He recalled this story many years later and said that the decision to change his thinking was a very easy one, but the discipline needed to change his addictive habit was much harder—to the point that a year or so after this encounter, such was his will power that cigarette smoke actually began to make him nauseous, and he couldn't stand to be in the presence of people who were smoking. The essence of this story is to seek the power of positive thought and the power of changing your mindset.

That mindset can serve you well in teaching if you really truly believe it. I'm not talking about just rolling with the punches and giving everything your best but truly believing that your life as a teacher is really having a positive influence on those you teach. This leads me to the thought of something that I've heard many times in my years as a teacher: in teaching, one cannot see the fruits of one's labour or the results of one's success immediately. I remember hearing this and thinking, *Well, how in the heck can we know if we are doing a good job or not?*

When I think about my life as a teacher in the past, and even my life as a teacher right at this present moment, the answer is that I just know. I know I've done a good job when I see all the young children I taught all those years ago grow into well-balanced and well-adjusted young adults. At the school I'm teaching at as I write this, I have the benefit of seeing this first-hand. I am a primary teacher in Cairns, Australia, and I have taught here for the last seventeen years, mostly as a preschool teacher. Now I am teaching at a school that has a high school across the road, so we are all part of the same college. I taught many of these preschool children at a few other schools, and now they are attending this high school across the road, as it is one of the local feeder schools. I have the supreme privilege of seeing all of those little bodies who were once my beloved preschool students now grown into young adults about to graduate from high school and watch them as they embark onto the next stage of their lives.

It brings tears to my eyes just writing this, as do the graduation ceremonies I get to attend with these students. I once told the parents of one of these students that the greatest honour I have ever felt as a teacher is to be there for a student's very first day of school. I was there to guide them and share the best of my teaching with them and to be there again on their very last day. Like I said, nothing beats that feeling.

If you stay the course and strive along on your journey as a teacher, you too can have magic moments like this that will last a lifetime. The fringe benefits to being such a legendary teacher are all the boxes of chocolate you can extract out of the students' parents for your tireless services rendered (but I think that's only really in primary school maybe.) So, yes, go the distance and stay the course with this.

The main theme to this teaching journey is to own it and make it yours. When I was in my first year of teaching all those years ago as a preschool teacher in a day care centre, I bought a banner from an educational store. It read: "Have the courage to be yourself." I've hung that banner at the front of every classroom I have ever taught in. I've told all of my students that if they only remember one thing that I ever taught them, then may it be the words on that banner. May they always remember to be themselves and to embrace their journey for itself. I would also say, "Be yourself, as you are the only one who can do it."

I encourage you as a teacher or even as a student teacher or even as a parent or even as a mentor just to be who God intended you to be. Don't walk in anyone else's shadow or be dominated by anyone else's opinion about who you are or who you can become. This gets back to that issue of self-esteem and self-belief and how our society or culture or whatever deems to indoctrinate people with advertisements for products and images of supposedly beautiful or successful people. Be your own person. Be the teacher/mentor/role model that you would love to have. Because at the end of the day, if you can't inspire yourself, how will you ever be able to inspire others?

This reminds me of another story, of a woman I once knew named Carol. I taught Carol's son many years ago in preschool, and I told Carol that she was the bravest woman I had ever met. You see, Carol was a very attractive and beautiful woman, and then one day she was badly burnt in a house fire. As Carol described it to me, it was God's way of telling her not to rely on her looks for self-worth. Carol spent a long time in hospital and underwent dozens of operations on her body. When I met her, she was very badly scarred. But she had this aura about her that spoke volumes. She would come into the preschool and talk to the young children about her ordeal and about how much stronger it had made her a person.

I remember seeing Carol at a function a few years later and greeting her with a big hug and a kiss. Someone asked me who she was and why was I hugging and kissing her, as she had such a badly disfigured face. I was at first perplexed and replied that this was my inspirational friend Carol and we were like family, and I always greeted the people I loved this way. Then it occurred to me that this person only saw Carol for what she looked like, not who she really was underneath all of those scars.

This story reinforces the overwhelming privilege I've had of being acquainted with fantastic people like Carol. That is the pinnacle of my teaching journey, when I have been open to learning from those I have encountered whilst being of service to teach others.

Another aspect of your teaching journey that you will need to develop is a sense of resilience. This will, like everything else, become stronger as you gain more experience and encounter many new situations. The key ingredient in developing your resilience is to undertake many different tasks within your teaching. Chopping and changing your approach is a fantastic way to gain more insight into this. Experimenting with different ideas and approaches once again can lead you to new roads of possibility within your teaching journey.

For myself, I have always studied the legendary teachers and learnt from their methods. Like all gurus, they are more than happy to share their ideas and expertise with anyone willing to ask. Be brave, and be the kind of teacher who believes in making a difference not only to your students and the greater community but especially to yourself.

Your teaching journey will be full of many different types of experiences—some good, some great, and others not so. One of the best ways to remember the good and even great things that you experience with your students is to write them down. This is where a teaching journal comes in handy. It can be a fancy one or just a plain notepad. Whatever it is, it will become your memory of the past as you move forward on your teaching journey.

Some teachers may say that they are too busy or too tired at the end of the day to put their spare time into something like this. But I can tell you now that all the teaching journals I have kept over the years have become not only my memories but also a written history of myself and how I have grown and evolved as not only a teacher but a person. They are even helping me right this minute as I write this. Funnily enough, they are even helping me to remember other fantastic teaching experiences that I hadn't written down but are coming back to me.

The best thing about journals is that you get to own them but also the experiences they contain. This becomes even more valuable when reminiscing with your past students as they continue on their own journeys as adults. I have enough faith in you as a teacher that if you are reading this, you will go the distance and make teaching your lifelong career.

This notion of teaching being a journey has another important aspect that you will need to perfect (or at least become aware of), and that is the notion of walking the walk and talking the talk. This applies when you are dealing with your students, parents, or fellow teachers. You will need to be able to take on your teaching persona and really believe it for yourself. If you believe it, your students will pick up on your energy. This in turn will have a positive effect on all stakeholders you encounter day to day in your teaching life.

When you go out into the community, it's important to take this persona and energy with you. Be proud to announce that you are a teacher and that you are working in an important industry that is helping to shape the next generation. When you take this approach, you will discover not only how different it makes you feel but also how others treat and respond to you.

As a teacher, you will be required to give a lot of yourself in many ways. Acts of giving on your part will enable true miracles to occur within your teaching life. In a world that is obsessed with getting, the world of teaching needs more givers. Yes, there are plenty of giving teachers out there, and I applaud them; but there are also lots of takers. Giving promotes a sense of freedom and creates an environment where everybody wins. It also creates a sense of abundance where there are limitless resources, be it the physical kind or the creative kind.

Being a giver has brought me many miracles that I just can't explain. When others see you giving the best of yourself to your students or your school or institution, it inspires others to do so. Now as in all dealings with humans, you will meet some teachers who are hoarders—not hoarders as in they can't bear to throw anything away (though you will encounter them too) but rather hoarders who give off an energy of never having enough of anything or always making out that they have been short-changed. It is great to collect an abundance of physical resources in teaching, but be a good sharer. God and the Universe will then bless you with abundance I guarantee it.

Another way that this has become more than evident in my teaching life is my pay scale. I have never in my whole teaching career (twenty-two years thus far) ever asked for a promotion or pay raise in any way. But just as I love giving the best of myself to my students and to my school or institution, my pay has seemed to go up and up over the years without any input from me. Yes the teachers Union has obviously helped with this in a human way. But God and the universe have seen to it that all the great sharing, volunteering, and understanding I've done through my teaching has never gone unrewarded. And my current pay reflects this hugely.

I would like to reinforce this notion with a little story about how I became a senior teacher. After the required number of years in teaching, I received a letter from my employer stating that I was eligible to be promoted to senior teacher status. I took this letter to my then-principal and asked what it involved. He outlined a procedure of filling out the appropriate paperwork, and this would then be followed by a series of formal interviews. Upon being successful with all of this, I would receive a rather substantial raise in pay and be eligible for further promotions down the track. He asked if I wanted to begin this process and get the ball rolling, and I agreed.

A couple of months went by. I had almost forgotten about this discussion and the whole process when I was called back in to see the principal. Now just to add, the main point of being a giving teacher was that I had continued to do extra-curricular activities with many students and also made a point of being giving teacher to others in any way I could. The principal presented me with the paperwork all filled out on my behalf and asked for my signature on a few pages at the end. He then shook my hand and announced proudly that from this day forth, I was bestowed with the honour of being a senior teacher.

At this point, I felt a little bit puzzled as to why this process had been so quick and, to be honest, a little too easy. I questioned the principal about this, to which he replied that I was doing more in that school than most of the other teachers combined, and he really appreciated how many of the students (and also their parents) were directly benefitting from my altruistic approach to teaching. The key here was that with all the extra things I was doing and all the extra students I was helping, I never once sought recognition for myself or came from a place where I was owed something.

I have applied this principle to getting extra non-contact time in my teaching life. I can honestly say, as God is my witness, that I have never thought that I was owed extra time. Sure, in the day-to-day scheme of things in my teaching life, other things get in the way of some of our specialist lessons. There were times when my class would have to miss a music lesson due to a whole school performance practice or even a physical education (gym) class due to a school sports event. But I have always rolled with whatever God or the universe has brought my way. When specialist teachers come to me and announce rather apologetically that for whatever reason, our lesson for that day can't happen. I accept their news gracefully and make it known that I won't be keeping score on what my class has missed out on or how many hours I'm owed.

The amazing thing is that whenever there is some spare specialist time that appears, who do you think is at the top of their list? And even in the odd circumstance where the time is not convenient, I am always happy to just pay it forward and pass it on to another teacher who has been so kind as to give something to me. Actually, I have so many of these wonderful teachers in my current teaching life that I sometimes find it hard to choose. But the universal message is always the same: give and you will, in the teaching world, receive (and many times over).

Obviously, it's not about giving to get something in return, or even giving in the hope of getting things back tenfold. The best part is, when I give something to another person—whether it be a student, parent, or fellow teacher—I always feel a great sense of being on God's path for me. It reinforces that part of me that is proud to do things because they feel right and therefore feel good. I would encourage you to try this in your teaching life and to be constantly looking for more opportunities to be helping people and be proud to be a giving teacher.

If anyone ever scoffs at you for doing so and tells you that you're wasting your time, just do what Wayne Dyer instructs us to do in his many books: send them peace and love, and wish them all the best on their journey. Then add them to the top of your list of people to give to. Nothing brings me more joy than to give to people who never expect or even believe in it. Try it for yourself; you won't be disappointed.

Your teaching life will take you to places you obviously don't want to go, either physically or emotionally, but that's where the true treasure is. Rise above and beyond your fears and apprehensions to where, as a teacher, you are meant to be. If you ever meet any legendary teachers in your time, they will tell you the exact same thing. There is no reward in being comfortable, and there is no prize for trying to find convenient situations within which to teach. Be open to where your higher power wants you to go, and be open to a greater sense of higher learning within yourself. Your teaching journey can and will be as unique as you wish to make it.

The best encouragement I can give you is to be brave, be bold, and keep expanding your mindset as your teaching journey progresses. You'll be amazed at the number of fantastic opportunities that will suddenly and mysteriously appear before you. Go with this, have faith, trust in your own abilities, and enjoy the ride.

CHAPTER 4

SHARE THE POWER

ONE BOOK I can highly recommend to any teacher, new or experienced, is *Building Classroom Discipline* by C. M. Charles. I came across this book whilst studying at university way back when, and it has become my bible of how to interact with my students and, as the title states, build classroom discipline.

Now, there are plenty of books around that can tell you how to teach or even suggest to you how to teach well. But ultimately, it all comes down to your interactions with your students. There are as many different teaching approaches as there are teachers. Just like cooking a steak or rearing a child, there is no right or wrong way to go about it. Some practices will bring great benefits to all stakeholders involved, and some won't.

As a teacher, whether new or experienced, you will come across thousands of ideas and concepts on how to effectively run a classroom. The one principle that I have learnt in my teaching travels is to share the power with your students. Now please don't misunderstand my motives here. This is not about handing over power to your students in any way, shape, or form. They should not have the power, because as your students, they are not yet equipped to handle the responsibility that goes with it. This is why they are the students. Sharing the power is about you still being the boss but giving your students the privilege of being under your guidance. You should think highly enough of yourself to want to share this power and thus collaborate to make teaching and learning a team effort.

I explain to my students that I am always the boss, and that I am always holding all of the cards. If they want some of the cards, they need to be part of the team. I also tell them that I am the coach of our team and that if they want me to help them to bring out their best, we need to work together. It's a collaborative relationship where teachers and learners work together to share ideas and opinions about what needs to be taught and to be learnt.

C. M Charles outlines how forming relationships with your students is the cornerstone of effective teaching and learning. At my current school, there has been a heavy emphasis on this by our admin. To their credit, there have been some remarkable situations where students have taken active responsibility for not only their learning but their attitude towards learning.

Another aspect that goes into effective teaching is order and rules. Every experienced teacher knows this, and every new teacher needs to learn this for it to assist you in your classroom. Rules are what govern what is acceptable and what is not acceptable.

It has been suggested to me as a teacher in previous years that one's classroom should only have about five or so rules. These rules should be basic and to the point about students' behaviour and the teacher's expectations. Any more than five or so, and students can become overwhelmed and begin to stress about not conforming or become so overwhelmed they choose to not conform altogether.

These rules should be written out at the beginning of a school year or whenever a new class begins. This should be done in consultation with the students so that they get to contribute to how the class is run. They get to own the rules and be part of the governing of their little universe that they are being educated in. This is what is meant by sharing the power.

Another aspect of this is for your students to suggest what would be their punishment for not following the rules. I like to give my students a chance to defend their position if need be, because as a teacher (and an imperfect human being) I have dealt out punishment without knowing all the facts and have looked very foolish at times as a result. Share the decision-making, especially with young children.

At times, I have even asked a victim of a minor classroom offense to state the punishment for the perpetrator. Nothing brings more joy to a young child than getting to dish out punishment to a classmate. Believe me, they are ruthless with each other, sometimes to the point where I have to step in and dull down the punishment, much to the relief of the student on the receiving end. This also allows me, the teacher, to build up a few bonus emotional bank-account points on some students to use in the future when required. Believe me, they will always be required at some point in the future.

One of my greatest teaching mentors was a man named Darral. He was to me the complete teacher. He had an early childhood teaching degree like me and primarily taught in the junior grades of primary (elementary) school. His dedication to his students was unmatched by anybody. Establishing a good rapport with his students was one of his highest priorities. His ability to share the power with his students was built on mutual respect and understanding that was held in high regard by all, especially his students.

I would also like to mention another mentor I had the good fortune to come across when I was a junior teacher. His name was Colin, and he was a teacher mentor and behaviour specialist. I will never forget what Colin said to me one day after observing my preschool teaching. He said, "Adam, if you can consciously build up a good emotional bank account with these students, then you don't really ever need to worry about classroom behaviours." He then reassured me that I was well on the way to doing this, and he had all confidence in me becoming an outstanding teacher.

In *How to Set Limits* by Elizabeth C. Vinton MD. She outlines the most crucial guidelines that all children and students should know, including who the boss is and what the rules are. I have come back to these words many times over the years, and they never ever seem to lose their potency. Even though this advice is so simple, so elementary, it encapsulates everything I believe a great teacher, mentor, and role model should have: the ability to set rules and then to enforce them appropriately. It's the old expression of, "Say what you mean and mean what you say."

This is where consistency comes to the fore of any great classroom. Consistency must be the crucial element in the fairness of your classroom. Children are obsessed with the notion of fairness. Their whole world revolves around someone not getting more than them. This is the be-all and end-all of their existence. To be on a level playing field is the main focus of all students of any age, and knowing that the rules apply to everyone involved in the same way gives them sense of trust that they are safe in that world. If they feel safe, then they will feel valued. They are valued as contributor to not only their own education but to the education of others.

Another great point in Vinton's book is that social skills are the main component of a healthy and confident child. Expand this notion to all students under your command, whether they be young children, teenagers, or adults. The teaching of social skills can pave the way for the highest standard of interaction possible for all stakeholders in your classroom. The social skills platform is no different from following the rules. Whatever you expect will be delivered.

It's like universal magnetic attraction: whatever standard you seek, that's exactly what you'll get. The universe that is your classroom will adhere to your precise wishes, either positive or negative. If you expect a certain level of classroom behaviour, you need to make sure you have the tools and procedures to back it up. If these fail, you will need a backup plan for your backup plan.

Another tool in my teaching repertoire is to let students imagine they are going to miss out on something special. This could be a game or an in-class reward. I would give another student options for how this would be administered. Suddenly, every student wanted to be in on the action, and every student wanted to be chosen to select the classroom reward. When all else fails, just go back to good old-fashioned threats. They work every time. (Just joking ... kind of.)

With power-sharing comes an even greater responsibility that you will undertake as teacher. That is the concept of being popular with your students. Please don't misunderstand this concept. Like any other human being, I like to have my ego stroked. But for some strange reason unknown to science, and perhaps known only to God, this is the greatest fear of some teachers. Some see being popular as being soft, and others seem to deem it inappropriate.

I have considered all of these aspects and have found that being popular is not a bad thing. Yes, I do admit that I have been soft on some students. And I am quite happy to admit that those students got soft treatment because they did not make my life hard. I have even gone so far as to explain this to other students who didn't understand why this was happening. I would point out that their inappropriate behaviour was getting them the negative attention that they had requested. In the future, if they wanted positive attention, it would require from them some appropriate behaviour.

In my classrooms, I have quite often given so many options for positive behaviour that the students forgot about wanting to participate in negative behaviour patterns. When you ask students (mainly young children in my case) what it is they want, they have no problem telling you. When you can share the power with them and give them options as to what's possible as far as rewards go, you have them in the palm of your hand. Of course, you as the teacher still need to give them a generous if only occasional dose of consequences for inappropriate behaviours. But by developing a good rapport with your students, you will inevitably be able to gauge where they are going and what course of disciplinary action is needed to keep them on that course.

This is where consistent reminders of classroom rules come into play. Remember to follow through on any course of action. As a new teacher, you will realise that any threat made to your students must be followed through on for you to maintain your position at the top.

If you say it, then you have to mean it. If you mean it, then it has to happen. If it doesn't happen, your status with your students will drop faster than a lead balloon.

Walk the walk and talk the talk, over and over again, until you're sure they got the message. And then give them a gentle reminder just so they know you're still the boss. With young children, just tell it like it is. They'll understand, believe me.

Extending further into this subject of sharing the power is the concept of honesty with your students. A very important part of sharing your power is the ability to be honest about the journey they will undertake in this learning process. As a teacher, your professionalism is always going to be your highest priority, yet this does not take away your ability as a person and as a human to share more honesty with your students.

For example, if you are tired, admit this to your class. Create a discussion around what makes teachers tired. Extend this into a discussion about what makes the students themselves tired also. This will give you, their teacher, a different perspective into what makes them tick and how they are perceiving you and your teaching. The students are all very much aware of these answers and will be totally honest with you in their responses.

I have always found it interesting how many teachers do not seem to care for their students' opinions on anything. Remember that a student's mind is not a pot to be filled but rather a fire to be ignited. The students are our clients who we need to get constant feedback from. Note that I did not state that we have to keep them happy, but rather give them our best knowledge and expertise to allow them to succeed. This I have found has created over the years a greater understanding between myself and my students.

I don't ever make excuses for being tired in my teaching job (as this is almost a constant thing), but rather, I allow my students to own that little part of themselves they truly understand. The same goes for when you are feeling negative stress or hungry or worried or whatever. Not that you go and share your life story with your students, but in small ways, you allow them to see your human side so that they may learn to understand you as their teacher better.

This all may seem very out there and revolutionary, but I have been doing this for years and have created some fantastic bonds with my students, and I have observed many other legendary teachers doing the same in their teaching roles, either consciously and or subconsciously. As I always tell my students, our journey together is a team effort. I am obviously the commander and chief of the classroom, but they have equally their own important role to play in the teaching in learning process.

I constantly remind all the students I have ever taught that I am there exclusively for them. I also let them know that as a professional, I get paid for it, but they (especially young children) can see dedication in any adult at twenty paces. Their little internal genuineness radars pick up your energy or vibe long before you even open your mouth.

Along with honesty, give your students a small emotional escape valve, a little "out" from the day-to-day craziness of the classroom. I recall few years back having a conversation about this with my mother, who was also a legendary teacher. She said that I should never emotionally corner a student on anything, even when I know I am 100 per cent right. She said to let students know very clearly that you don't tolerate or reward negative behaviour or disrespect, but you are willing to meet them halfway and allow them to negotiate their own path into making positive decisions for themselves.

Unfortunately, I didn't take this advice at first and selfishly prided myself on emotionally dragging a few of my students over the proverbial coals. The lesson I learnt very quickly was how this can seriously affect a student's self-esteem and self-worth when it comes from one of the best role models they look up to so much. I am happy to say that I have remedied this and have realised the error of my ways. The key here as a teacher is to never embarrass students in front of their peers. There can be humour between you, and of course friendly banter, but as the teacher, there is a very fine line between asserting your authority and tipping a student over the edge with negative behaviour.

In a parting thought on this subject, I would suggest that you experiment with this for yourself in your classroom. Identify any points of interest with this with your students and promote discussions around it. Above all, don't forget to keep having fun as you teach. Believe me, your students will always appreciate this.

Stephen Covey, in his book *Primary Greatness*, describes how most leaders do not want to share power with subordinates. They do not wish to give the keys to the inmates. But as teachers and as leaders of our students, this is essential for real lasting trust and relationships to take form. Without mutual trust, your words and actions as a teacher (and role model) are going nowhere. Sharing the power with your students creates a win–win situation where everyone involved can be a part of the approach while at the same time working for common and individualised goals. That is to say, whatever you are teaching will not take on a robotic-type tone, with the students only retaining the basics without letting the real messages soak in.

Show that you are passionate and be bold enough to experiment with this concept of sharing. The unfortunate aspect of many teachers' approaches is that they are too scared to experiment. The main goal of your teaching should always be to provoke thought, not to just follow guidelines and procedures.

Of course, teachers of all kinds are bound by a curriculum, but nothing says you can't make it your own and then allow your students to make it their own also. Of course, this takes courage on a grand scale, and unfortunately, you may be met with resistance. Teaching is one profession where being an individual thinker and a brave soul is not necessarily frowned upon but not really embraced either.

In the thought-provoking movie *Conrack*, the character of Pat Conroy, played by Jon Voight, is given the task of teaching a group of impoverished black students in America's Deep South. He soon realises that he needs to break away from traditional teaching methods to get his message across to his students. Robin Williams's character of John Keating does the same in the film *Dead Poets Society*. Unfortunately for both of these characters, it costs them their teaching jobs. But in the real world, I have seen many legendary teachers weave their own little bits of magic into curricula and practices whilst still being able to follow the standards set.

Sometimes this is how educational change comes about. My teacher friend named Danielle has this beautiful saying on one of her paperweights: "The best teachers teach from the heart and not by the book." Those few words have summed up my whole approach. They lead me day by day as I work towards becoming a legendary teacher along with those who are brave enough and clever enough to know the system and to be leaders into new areas of thought within education.

We are much like the prisoners of war in Paul Brickhill's famous novel *The Great Escape* (and the film that was made from it). The prisoners knew that they were under constant observation by the Nazis, yet they became masters of disguise, letting their captors know that they weren't ever going to give in. The object was always to look like you were being good or doing the right thing, but the reality was very different.

Effective and courageous teaching involves sharing knowledge with your students in a way that can be disguised as other things— or at least those other things can once again be woven into practices and procedures to promote different ways of approaching concepts and solving problems. The Nazis (not literally) in this case are your admin or supervisors, and the captives or POWs are you and your students (once again, not literally speaking … much!). You and your students are not being sneaky or deceptive towards your superiors but rather engaging in a practice that you can once again own and therefore learn to love.

Being bold in teaching is not about breaking any rules but manipulating the rules in such a way that all of you can own your own part, teachers and students alike. The best legendary teachers I have ever known knew how to add the human element to their classroom and school rules. Many times, teaching will require you to make decisions based not on the rules as such but on what is the right thing to do given that particular situation. I've had students query me on why I have altered the rules for different students, and I confidently explain how rules can be modified to suit a particular person or situation. As the boss of the classroom, I have to be very much aware of how my decisions can affect others.

Humility is another huge factor that can take you a long way with your students. Most of my students seem to think that as a teacher, I know everything. With preschoolers, this is very easy to get away with, but with older students not so much. Sure, I would joke about it in jest with my older students over the years, but essentially I would at different points be completely perplexed by some word or topic or answer to a problem. The best thing I have ever done is to be humble enough in front of my students to admit that I didn't know something or kind of knew something but wasn't sure and had to look it up.

At times, I have even made a game out of it and taken out the dictionary and raced the students to see who could find the meaning of a word first. Nothing will get your students interested in something faster than racing against the teacher to find something first. This can also be done with a thesaurus or an atlas or any kind of educational textbook.

The best part of this is that when we're done, I ask my students what valuable lesson they have learned, and they always give the same answer: how to use their brain to find information for the sole purpose of becoming more informed and educated. And yes, I do admit (as most teachers would) that if I really don't know something, I will google it. This word has become synonymous with researching or looking up pretty much anything in our known world. As much as I do use it in the classroom with my students, I try to make it the last resort. I tell my students that I prefer they look it up in books first.

Another valuable aspect of sharing the power is the way you treat your teacher aides (or teacher assistants). Sharing the power with your aides is one of the most valuable practices you will ever use in your classroom. By sharing the power, I mean that you give them autonomy and emotional space in which to work. Sure, it's good to establish your teaching expectations with them straight up, but also be willing to listen to their ideas and ask them where there might be gaps in your teaching routine. Ask them lots of questions about what they see in your classroom and how things can be improved and modified to best suit your students.

Some aides may be taken aback by such an approach, since you as the teacher are the boss in charge. But two sets of eyes are always better than one, especially when it comes to delivering quality education on a day-to-day basis. Besides, aides are the only adults who see you teach and interact with your students every day, not just occasionally. At some point, you will need their help. Building a good working relationship is a very smart practice.

Teacher aides are the educational nurses to you, the educational doctor, in the theatre of educational operations. In my experience, it has paid handsomely to treat these people like royalty, as they are in many ways your best source of ideas and resources. Let me repeat that again in a way you the reader won't easily forget: treat your teacher aides like royalty, because in your classroom, they are.

I have had countless teacher aides over the years but one has always stood out from all the others. Her name was Julie and she was my classroom teacher aide when I first came to teach preschool here in Cairns many years ago. Julie was one of those people who just seemed to know something ten minutes before it actually happened. Over the time we worked together I would always ask for her opinion on most things and she somehow always seemed to know the right course of action. Of course she would always remind me that as the teacher I was responsible for making the important decisions but I never did anything before I consulted her first. And the best thing was that all of our preschool students would see this high level of consultation between us. They knew that I didn't need to behave like a dictator to get things done. They would see high quality conversation and respect being conducted by us right before their very eyes. And Julie and I became best friends and today I even claim her more like part of my extended family. She has been one of the best positive influences in my teaching life (and my life in general too).

And again most of the teacher aides I've had the privilege of working with over the years have been parents of students I have taught, or at least have had children go through that particular school at some point. Since most of these aides are also women (and mothers), I have always trusted their natural maternal instincts as to what is the best way of doing things. They pretty much see everything—including things I miss. When you can identify your aides' strengths and work with these, you will strike pure gold.

The best part about working within your aides' strengths is that you can create a fantastic energy where you work in sync (as I did with Julie). This is a feeling in teaching that I just can't describe. It's like having an extra set of hands and an extra pair of eyes that are just an extension of you and your teaching. And to work out your teacher aides' strengths is very simple. All you need to do is sit down with them and ask them what skills and interests they have and how they feel they could contribute these to improve the overall well-being of the classroom and the students.

You will obviously encounter some teacher aides who are bossy or have a natural tendency to take over, but as long as you keep the lines of communication open and are willing to meet them where they are at, things should go okay. They are people just like you, with feelings, hopes, fears, and all the rest, and they just want to be treated with respect and dignity.

Before making crucial decisions about anything to do with a student or my classroom or with a particular tricky lesson, I consult my aides. They very much appreciate being given a chance to add input into the situation, and quite often they can offer a different opinion from a different angle. As most of them have a wealth of worldly experience, it pays to tap into that knowledge and see what other ideas could come from this.

Another great payoff for being nice, kind, and respectful to your teacher aides is that any spare time they have, they will be happy to help you with little jobs that need to be done or with extra support for your students. I can proudly say that I have never asked for any extra teacher aide time for my students, even though some of them desperately needed it. Instead, I have always given my aides the best possible situation within which to work, and the power of the divine universe rewards me with all the extra help I have ever needed and then some.

I'll share a little story about this from a little while back. I was about to hold an end-of-semester class party for a grade 1 class I was substituting in. I was faced with a class of twenty-five six-year-olds staring at a mountain of party food that was about to send their energy levels into the stratosphere. I was a little concerned about how to go about this on my own, especially since I hadn't really had time to develop a good rapport with the students. I just stood there, opened my arms slightly, and quietly prayed to God and to the universe for any help with this situation, as I really needed it.

About a split second later (and it really was a split second, believe me), a spare teacher aide walked into the room and said that she was with this class for the rest of the morning. I didn't even have time to blink, let alone give thanks, when another teacher aide came through the door offering to help out for the session. As if this wasn't enough, a third teacher aide came to the door offering some assistance if we needed it also. I asked all three of them to please prepare the food, and I would do crowd control.

With this unbelievable help from the divine, everyone involved had a great time, and the aides all told me that this was the best class party they had ever attended. I naturally in turn lavished them with praise and let them know that it was only a fantastic success because of their generous help. I know that if any more assistance is needed for anything, the universe will definitely be sending it my way.

This leads me to the subject of how to host a legendary class party. As these parties are held at the end of the term or semester or school year, you and your students are generally physically and emotionally tired from your workload. This generally means that your patience and your capacity for clarity is somewhat hampered. I have known of a few teachers who do not have any kind of celebration to mark the ending of the school term, semester, or year because it's just too hard to deal with. This has always struck me as a bit selfish, because as teachers, we are role models who must be able to celebrate any small successes with our students, especially the conclusion of a significant period of teaching and learning time.

A successful class party where everybody gets maximum benefit with a minimum of craziness requires a couple of crucial elements. The first is to announce the party well in advance so that your students have something to work towards. Some teachers do this about a month in advance, but for me, a couple of weeks is fine. This allows your students to know what's going on without them focusing too far into the future.

Next, specify what types of foods you want at the party itself. You can go for the pot-luck approach, which gives students a choice of what they would like to bring. Or you can make a chart and place food suggestions on it, and then ask your students which food they would like to bring from the choices. You can even go for party food themes, such as a Mexican taco party or a Japanese sushi party, where the students can either bring the food ready-made or you can have a cooking lesson followed by the party itself. Cooking lessons with younger children are a great idea but will require extra help from teacher aides or accompanying parents.

The next factor that goes into a successful class party is to give the students a sense of inclusion on whether the party will happen. There may be a bit of bribery involved and even a few threats of being excluded from the party should any student's behaviour not be up to appropriate standards. In twenty plus years of teaching, I have never had a student willingly miss out on a class party. Make it sound fun and exciting (because it is), and no one will want to miss out on the action.

Just a note on the party food again: limit the amount of sugary foods. Yes, it's a celebration, and students—especially young children—love to eat anything completely laced with sugar, but keep a check on this. Allocate certain foods to certain students, and be very specific about the amounts to be brought in. This way, you know exactly what is coming into your classroom, how much of it should be consumed, and what effect it may have on the students' well-being.

Crowd control during a class party can make or break your sanity as a teacher. Be very clear about your classroom rules and any consequences that will occur should anyone's behaviour become inappropriate. Place the food on classroom tables in the centre of your classroom. If you have any teacher aides or parents helping, please ask for their assistance in preparing or unwrapping the food. Mums will automatically go into hostess mode and begin without even being asked. Once again I am always in awe of their natural instincts.

Seat the students in a large circle around the food tables with enough room to move easily between them (for students who may need to leave the room for washing hands or toileting purposes). Place all available rubbish bins (trash cans) right next to the tables to reduce the need for students to travel too far to place scraps or food waste into them.

Sit the students down and insist on silence. This may take a little bit of prompting, as their eyes will be on the food and not on you. But be very insistent that they not only listen to your party rules but look at you whilst you explain them. Advise your students that they must not get out of their seats until instructed. Advise them that they will be signalled to move by being pointed at, so they know to keep their eyes on you. This also means that they will need to stay silent, because they don't want to miss out. Advise them that any student making noise or talking will be chosen to go last (this works, believe me).

Reward any high-behaviour students by choosing them somewhere in the middle; if you choose them last, they will quite often get upset and refuse to participate. This also can sometimes give them a complex about not being included. I have made all these mistakes overs the years, so I am only speaking from a place of experience, not perfection.

Instruct the students to wash their hands thoroughly before eating. If a sink is not easily available then use portable hand sanitiser instead. Then instruct students selected to take one piece of food for each hand and return to their seat to eat it. Be very strict about touching food and eating it. I always advise my students that if they touch it, then they're going to eat it. Occasionally, this can spark a tantrum, as young children love to touch everything first to get a real feel for it before it goes into their mouth. This is mainly a tactile experience for them, but just warn them that this is not a sensory activity, and if they don't want to eat it then they had better not touch it. This can also be accompanied with a time out warning. This again will get their attention immediately.

The same goes for any students who take one bite of something they thought they liked but suddenly change their mind. You can advise them to throw it away, but it comes with a five-minute time penalty. They must sit and not go up for the next batch of food for five minutes. It's amazing how students can eat something when they know they may have to serve out a penalty for any length of time, especially when everyone else is still eating.

Specify that with chips (crisps), students can take a small handful instead of just one chip. Many students have to overcome huge mental dilemmas over this rule. When each handful of food has been consumed and properly swallowed, advise each student to sit silently once again and wait to be pointed to before beginning the second round of indulgence.

If any student forgets to bring something to a class party, there are a few things you can do. Notice I said *can* do, not *should* do. If students forget to bring something and you know that they are just forgetful, they can serve their penalty by waiting till everyone has had their fill and then eat after that. This may sound harsh, but on the occasions that students do this, they must be made aware of the fact that this does not entitle them to a free ride with the food at the expense of the students who have genuinely contributed. Warn your students of this rule beforehand so that even the parents are aware of the consequences. This will save you a few headaches with parent complaints later on.

There may also be students whose families simply cannot afford to send something for the party. As a teacher, I have always found it beneficial to buy a few extra food items myself and either give them to these students to contribute or announce that this is their contribution to the class as a whole. Don't make a big deal about it, as nothing hurts a student's self-esteem more than not being able to contribute to the class in any way, no matter how small it may seem.

Now with students coming back for seconds, thirds, fourths, fifths, sixths, and sometimes even beyond that, just use your discretion. Some students will eat till they make themselves sick. I have had a few of them over the years end up in sick bay with a raging stomach ache and an exaggerated story about when they should have stopped eating. Tell students in your pre-party instructions that if they feel full, they should stop eating.

Don't be too worried about extra food or leftovers. These can easily be consumed later in the day, either by your students or another class. I have yet to meet any student at any school who will decline leftover party food from anywhere. Walk around the school if you have to with any leftovers, and you'll be amazed how quickly they will disappear.

Another very important aspect of being a legendary teacher is to get to know your support staff. These are the people who do all the unseen—and in many cases unrecognised—yet vital work in your school. They are your cleaners, gardeners, and maintenance staff. Besides your teacher aides, they are among the best sources of information and support during your time in a school. These people work behind the scenes and are great sources of information on how to keep you classroom tidy, find extra pieces of useful furniture, or even acquire hard-to-get or free items like extra paper, cardboard, paint, and glue. Their knowledge and expertise will greatly enhance your ability to develop your public relations skills.

Get to know your cleaners on a first-name basis and get to know a little bit about them as people. In Dale Carnegie's iconic book *How to Win Friends and Influence People*, his overall theme is get to know someone's name and be able to spell and pronounce it properly. I'm not talking about false sincerity here, as people can generally see straight through that. Be genuine in your approach and be sincere about your dealings with these and pretty much everyone associated with your classroom. Your cleaners are people just like you, with feelings, hopes, dreams, and fears. And in my opinion, they do the most important yet most underrated job in your school, and that is to make it brand-spanking clean and tidy every day of the school year.

One thing I have learned in working with cleaners over the years is that when you show them the respect and appreciation they deserve, it will pay off tenfold in their loyalty and dedication to you and your students. The ability to make another person feel important is a skill that you as a teacher cannot do without. Your cleaners are generally older and have a wealth of lifetime experience in many areas just waiting for you to enjoy and learn from. In most cases, they are also parents, which makes them a valuable sounding board for how to deal with difficult issues with your students (and their parents too).

Another important aspect to making your cleaners feel valued is to make their lives easier. I do this by training my students, no matter what age group, to clean and tidy up their mess each and every day before home time. The simplest way to do this is to insist on the classroom looking exactly the way it did at the start of the school day. I tell my students that I'm not really concerned with how much mess gets made during the school day (as mess is their specialty), but I insist that it not be there when they leave for the day. I don't expect perfection, but I do expect commitment to at least showing the cleaners respect by limiting the time they need to spend each day in my classroom.

I have invited our cleaners to come into the classroom and give the students an opportunity to put a name to a face and be privileged to meet those who do the cleaning and after-hours work. When students are faced with a real person who has a very busy job of cleaning their school, this allows for a greater amount of understanding and compassion. The cleaners, in turn, are always appreciative of being allowed to feel part of the team and part of the students' education.

Another way to keep your classroom clean and tidy is to have brooms, dustpans, and even Dustbusters (mini vacuum cleaners) always readily available for students to use. Nothing says more to your students about commitment to keeping their classroom clean and tidy than letting them own their responsibility to this. When the equipment is close and ready to use, they can be trained to know exactly what to do. You can even make these into classroom jobs each week and throw in a few little bribes just for good measure.

When students are encouraged to become part of the cleaning staff, very few say no or want to miss out on the feeling of being important and being part of the classroom team. As a teacher, it is vitally important that you be a great role model and be seen cleaning up the occasional mess that is not yours also—especially something like spilled food or even vomit. Students see and absorb everything you do, and as a leader, you will need to get your hands dirty from time to time to show how things are done, and done properly. This is like gold when your students are asked to clean up something, as they know you have either done it yourself many times or are in there with them helping also.

The same applies to getting to know gardeners and maintenance staff. If you need anything in your classroom repaired and replaced promptly and with a smile, these are the people you must keep in good stead. Once again, I don't ever advocate that you show false sincerity. People can see straight through this in an instant, and even if it is their job to do something for you, you could easily find your classroom job fall mysteriously to the bottom of the to-do list. Be sincere, get to know them by name, and get to know a little bit about them.

Some of my cleaners, gardeners, and maintenance staff have, over the years, become my best friends. They have access to a wealth of resources in the school that others don't. If I ever find them giving me extra help (which is quite often), I always make it known that I will owe them a favour in return. This has allowed me, during my time as a teacher, to develop some fantastic horse-trading skills with the different departments. I can generally acquire, swap, or trade useful resources with other teachers or support staff within the school.

Take the initiative and watch how wonderful things can develop and grow between you, your workmates, and of course, your students. As with the cleaners, invite your gardeners and maintenance staff into your classroom to meet your students. Get them to talk to your class about having pride in your school and explain how keeping the school looking good is a team effort, which should very much include your students. This builds a better sense of community and belonging for everyone involved.

CHAPTER 5

TOOLS OF THE TRADE

A S WITH ANY profession, teaching requires a specific set of tools to get the job done. These tools can take many forms. Some are physical, some mental, some spiritual, and some metaphorical. The key is to know how to use the right tool for the right situation at the right time. This obviously takes a lot of practice, and you are going to make a lot of mistakes getting this right.

As a teacher, you will need to embrace your inhibitions and fears and accept that mistakes are part of the job. Ultimately, they will teach you the most about what type of teacher you are and, more importantly, what kind of teacher you want to become. This principle applies to new and experienced teachers alike, because in a lot of ways, that's all teaching really is: a series of steps towards self-renewal, over and over again. Perhaps the most important tool in your teaching toolkit is the mindset that change is inevitable, and you will need a very healthy dose of it year after year to keep yourself fresh and optimistic.

Now at this point, you may be thinking, *Who does this guy think he is? Has he ever seen my school or class or students? How can I accomplish this kind of stuff? Man, I just have to survive each day with my sanity intact and pray for the next to work out the same.* I respond to this way of thinking (which I have encountered within myself many times) with the words of the great industrialist Henry Ford: "If you think you can or you think you can't, either way, you're right." If you choose to stock your teaching toolkit with lots of negativity and pessimism, that's what will confront you. But if you choose to stock it with optimism, positivity, and hope, you are equipped with a very different approach.

The most difficult aspect of teaching, especially for new teachers, is the notion that there is a specific way things are done in a particular school or learning institution. Remember that there are always as many ways to teach as there are teachers. No approach, procedure, or learning situation is ever set in stone. New and beginning teachers out there, don't ever feel that you have to conform to anyone else's ideals. Learn from the positive and inspirational experienced teachers, as their guidance will always serve you well. Be respectful of their views. But don't feel that you have to agree with them, or at least not all of them.

Feel your way through your teaching career much the same way a rock climber feels the way up a cliff. Experience will tell you that you are going to fall sooner or later. The impact of that fall is governed by how well you have prepared yourself and how well anchored to the cliff face you are.

Another tool for your teaching toolkit is to celebrate and applaud other teachers' success. Nothing eats away at a teacher like a sense of professional jealousy. This can bring down any teacher, class, school, or learning institution. Yes, others will use your ideas, sometimes without your permission. But every experienced teacher knows that there are very few original ideas. Most are rehashed, repackaged, and reprocessed in one way or another. Remember that you as teachers are always on the same team. Ideas are to be shared and modified however you see fit.

Add your own sprinkle of magic to something. Give ideas to your students about how they may wish to adapt something into their own learning. You'll be pleasantly surprised with the results. Be open and willing to share every idea you have. Nothing is off limits.

The most experienced and legendary teachers are more than happy to share their ideas. Embrace their wealth of knowledge and know that one day, you will be in the position to pass valuable knowledge on to someone else.

This also relates to physical resources also. Be a good sharer. Share your paper, paint, glue, textbooks or whatever with others. Yes, you will meet some teachers who are greedy and will abuse your generosity with this. But they are a very small minority in the teaching game. Live in an abundant teaching universe and always know that the teaching supplies that you will ever need day-to-day will always be there. It's great to store certain items for different uses down the track but try not to just hoard things just for the sake of it. In my teaching journey I have donated whole cupboards and storerooms full of resources to other teachers and the faithful universe has never ever let me down. And later on when I really needed something it just seemed to appear out of nowhere (remember the teacher aide time stories).

You probably in many cases won't get back the same things or from the same person but like I keep saying, the universe will always reward you somewhere else or with something else. Any most importantly if you do begin to run out of storage space in your classroom, then this I believe is also the universe telling you to pay it forward to someone else. Experiment with this if you will and even make a game out of it. As with everything once again, you won't be disappointed.

This ties in with the previous chapter on sharing the power, as it allows your students to gain a greater sense of having something worthwhile to contribute in their classroom, especially right off the bat. I have yet to meet a human being who does not long for a sense of inclusion into a group or common cause. On the surface, many individuals (especially young children and teenagers) want to give the impression that they are a lone wolf and just don't care about anything. These are the ones who are especially craving a sense of inclusion and oneness with something they truly believe in. Give your students a slice of the rule-making decisions in your classroom, and this will allow you to move forward as a group.

If you are a contract or relief teacher and come into a classroom mid-term or mid-semester, your job of establishing yourself is obviously going to be a little more difficult. Once again, set your standards, and allow your students some room to negotiate these into an acceptable set of rules and expectations that suits the majority. You may get the odd student claiming that everything in this world is unjust and unfair, but just roll with it. These students are just testing the water, and if you set your acceptable standards and stick to them, they will gradually learn where they need to fit into these dynamics.

Just like all human beings, your students will push the rules and limits, sometimes to breaking point. That's OK, because as a teacher, you will need to expect this. When you give your students the right to express themselves and their opinions in an appropriate setting, this will lead to conflict at some point. It can lead to tension and a lot of questioning about how things are. In turn, this will allow your students to critically think for themselves and make their own decisions about what suits them. That is what you want to produce as a teacher: students who can make informed decisions that allow them to negotiate their way through the world.

Physical tools of the trade are things you will carry with you when you enter the classroom, wherever it is each day. The first thing I suggest you buy is a set of industrial-strength earplugs, especially if you are teaching young children. You will be confronted by noise of all kinds, especially those that don't go down well with your eardrums. These earplugs will save your hearing long-term. Industrial deafness does occur with teachers, so take precautions.

Earplugs can also be used in conjunction with a set of good-quality safety-rated industrial earmuffs. These come in particularly handy when you are attending a parade or assembly, and they are essential if not mandatory for any activity that involves music, such as a school dance or disco. Even lunch eating areas can get very noisy when you have large groups of students congregating together. You may look odd using these items, but your hearing will definitely thank you for it. Taking care of your hearing is a big part of your own well-being. It will speak volumes (pardon the pun) to your students about being healthy and having a good sense of self-respect.

Another physical tool in your teaching toolkit is a megaphone or portable microphone. This can either be belt-mounted or handheld. It can come in very handy when teaching hearing-impaired and special needs students and for other students with selective hearing (a lot of those around). It can be easily adjusted to suit how loud or soft you want your voice to be.

If you want to go high-tech (and more expensive), you could install a microphone-based sound system in your classroom. This can, however, irritate teachers near you, as your voice will carry a fair distance at times. Another very good complementary tool to this is to get some voice projection training. This can easily be done through investing in a good voice or acting coach. A singing teacher could also give you some very good foundational training in learning how to project your voice. Remember as a teacher your voice is your life and if it's gone then your livelihood can go with it.

Just to add another tool to your arsenal to help keep your voice in the teaching game, make up some saline mouthwash. Go to the supermarket or health food store and get yourself some good-quality rock salt. Put this into a small glass jar or bottle (it's a lot healthier than plastic). Add some filtered water to it and shake it up till all the salt is diluted. Have a little taste test, and if it has the consistency of seawater and seems totally undrinkable, you're right on the money. If not, just add some more salt.

Gargle a mouthful of this for five minutes or so each morning, and the same in the evening. It will not only keep your throat in good condition, but it will also do wonders for your nasal passages and sinuses and give your teeth and gums a good workout. Please be careful with this if you have high blood pressure, however, as the salt could aggravate your condition. Please consult your Doctor or Physician before doing this if you also have a pre-existing heart condition.

Protecting your voice is right up there with protecting your precious hearing. Your voice is there to be nurtured for the long haul. Look after it, as I have seen too many teachers have to retire early because their vocal chords just don't hold out. Be sensible. Even if you look silly doing these things and using these tools, who cares? No one is going give you back these things once they are gone or pay your medical expenses for you. If I've learned anything from my own teaching and my own life, it is that common sense is not that common. Be practical and be safe.

Another physical tool that is essential to becoming a legendary teacher is water. H_2O is the way to go. By this, I mean drink the stuff and make it a good habit to drink it regularly throughout your teaching day. A hydrated teacher is an effective teacher. A dehydrated one is not. If this will cause you to need to go to the toilet more, then so be it. Train your body when it's appropriate to go to the toilet and when it's not. You can actually do this, and it does work. If you want excuses, you'll find plenty; and by the same token, if you want practical and workable solutions, you can find them too. Like the saying goes, "Where there is a will, there is a way."

Whilst we are on the subject of consuming liquids throughout your teaching day, there are a few things you may not want to put into your system. I have been personally addicted to many of these substances, and if the truth be told, they are not really substances but addictive drugs, probably worse than any illegal kind. The saddest thing is that they are freely available in any quantity you want.

The first is Coca-Cola or any other caffeinated soft drink. This stuff is laced with so much caffeine and sugar it will not do you or your teaching day any good. The unfortunate thing about this is that most schools, colleges, universities, and other learning institutions have vending machines and cafeterias that pump this stuff out by the truckload. This is perhaps the one single addiction that is at epidemic proportions in this industry, among teachers and students alike. *But this is my go-to drink!* I hear you say. Well, change your go-to to a drink that cannot alter your mood or send your blood sugar level into hyperdrive. The correct answer is plain water. Once again, H_2O is the way to go.

That brings us to the next highly addictive and highly caffeinated drink: coffee. I hear the voices of thousands of teachers around the world screaming *"Nooooooooo!"* Coffee is the drug of choice for the teaching profession as a whole (and most other professions too). But my perception of a legendary teacher is not one who is drugged to the eyeballs on a highly caffeinated or sugar-laced beverage. And I must also add to this that no self-respecting, legendary teacher ever needs to consume energy drinks during their teaching day (or any other day for that matter).

If you are an avid fan of sugar-and caffeine-packed drinks, I urge you to really consider the damage these concoctions are doing to your body. As teachers, we are constantly horrified at how our students seem to consume these at any point in the school day, yet as adults, we seem to think it is OK to do so. Moderation or reduction is good as far as these drinks go, and eliminating them from your life altogether is even better.

I admit that both cola and coffee were once my go-to drinks. But I trained myself with sheer willpower (and help from lots of Wayne Dyer books) to kick these nasty habits. Or at least, I turned them into something that I didn't need to feel competent or even with it during my teaching day. Effective teaching requires you to have a clear mind (and a healthy body).

Now, I know this sounds like a huge task. As humans, we love our addictions. The old saying, "that's just the way I am" seems to reverberate around every corner. My solution is to get yourself a copy of Dr. Wayne Dyer's *Your Erroneous Zones* and study it like the Bible. This book will give you the necessary mental tools to overcome any negative addiction or negative behaviour pattern. It may be scary, but this is the path I divinely believe I was meant to take as a teacher (and a person) and obviously to get this message across. Be brave and kick these habits. You won't believe how good you will feel once you do.

If you are really struggling with a harmful substance addiction, please seek some professional help and get it sorted. Become the student or person you would be proud to have as a teacher and occasionally take your own advice. Another great book that may help you in your journey with addictions is Kelly McGonigal's *The Willpower Instinct*. This is a fantastic book that outlines the behaviours behind addiction and how you can apply them to your own life in a practical way. Once again I know that this may sound confrontational, but sometimes shock treatment is the only way to get people to either listen or at least take notice.

McGonigal's book also powerfully illustrates how the addictions or vices of our modern society have started to dictate our daily lives. If you find yourself needing a go-to substance or a fix to get you started at the beginning of your teaching day, this is not a good place to be. I say this from experience, as I have been there myself with a range of pick-me-ups to help me along. Believe it or not, you don't need them at any point in your teaching life, and you can have a more satisfying teaching journey without them.

This news will ultimately upset many companies whose business is selling you addictive products. Whole industries are built on this, with the sole purpose of making money at the expense of your health. You can obviously take any of this advice or completely ignore it; it's up to you. But as the rates of diabetes, cancers, and various other disorders are on the rise, I'll let them do the talking for me. Just ask any general practitioner what it is they treat the most, and they will tell you that a greater percentage of these disorders are completely preventable with the proper lifestyle choices.

And yes, these are choices. I have never seen a teacher buckle to peer pressure and begin to drink coffee just because everyone else is doing it. It's like people who need a smoke (cigarette) break. An unbelievably healthier alternative is to just take a fresh-air-and-chat break or a go-for-a-walk break or a drink-of-water break. There is always a healthier alternative, so be open to it.

Just for the record, I would like to state that no, I am not some kind of Puritan who does not believe in having treats of any kind. Like thousands of other teachers in this great nation of ours (and world in general), I love to eat chocolate. But this is a treat, and just like all treats, I have it in extreme moderation.

While we are on the subject of all things healthy, this also goes for the food you as a teacher consume. As a teacher, you are a role model and a mentor to others. If you lead an unhealthy lifestyle through the foods you consume, this can have a huge effect not only on your health but also on your students' perception of you.

A teacher's professional life is like a marathon, not a sprint. You want to be around for many years to come. You want to have not only a long and wonderful life but also a healthy one. Junk foods and fast foods are treats in life and nothing more. The KFC website here in Australia actually describes their food as being just that: a treat. For me, that's all it ever has been, even though it is among my favourite foods.

I have shared this information about myself with my students when doing health and well-being lessons, and it has really gone over well. Fast foods and junk foods are like any other source of pleasure in our lives: only good when taken in extreme moderation. The strangest thing about unhealthy food is that it's also relatively expensive compared to foods that can be eaten raw or cooked and prepared at home.

I'll leave you with this parting thought from this section: if you're offended by anything stated above, that's great. Perhaps my message has gotten through to you. Be wise and be healthy—or at least as healthy as possible. Let this be a reminder that your personal health is like the quote about the journey of a thousand miles. It always begins with a single step.

One of the most important tools you will ever need is rest. This can be coupled with sleep and of course relaxation. As many of our new and beginning teachers are generally younger in age, I cannot stress this enough. Not getting enough sleep will seriously inhibit your ability to be an effective teacher. You may have just graduated from university or college and may have just received your first pay cheque and are thinking you'd love to party on. As much as it's a very tempting thing to head for the nearest pub or bar, please think again. When you get older (and hopefully wiser), you will be as shocked as I was at how much money you can waste on going out. It's great to socialise and get out amongst friends and all that, but don't let a lack of sleep become a constant thing in your life, and save as much as you can for other important things, like travel and paying off a car or house.

You may hear stories about how other teachers never get to bed before midnight each and every night, but make sure that *you* do. Be sure that you get a minimum of eight good hours of sleep each and every night. Thank the good Lord for your weekend and school holiday sleep-ins too. Rest, relaxation, and proper sleep are all by-products of a healthy and well balanced life.

One thing that can help you with this is a fantastic bed. Spend the money and buy a quality bed, and you will begin to feel the difference. Because once you cut back on sleep, it will begin to affect every aspect of your life (just ask any new parents). Be sensible and know and respect your limits.

I would just like to add one other important aspect of sleep I have discovered as a teacher. In a discussion with a naturopath a year or so back, I was introduced to the idea of switching off the alarm part of my alarm clock. I tried this for a week or so and was amazed at how I could train my body clock to wake me up before I needed to. I trained myself just before I went to sleep to gently tap the side of my temple and either silently or out loud tell myself what time I wanted to wake up. My mind (and my body clock) has never let me down. As a teacher, this has allowed me to wake up feeling fresher and more alert and ready for my school day. I have even trained my mind to allow me to have a built-in snooze button for weekends and holidays. I just tell my mind "ten more minutes" or whatever, and I just go to it. I guarantee you, it works. Experiment and play with this concept any way you like.

A tool that is just as important as sleep is relaxation. Now, lying on a beach somewhere on a deserted island is obviously a good place to start, but save those interludes for weekends and holidays. What I'm talking about here is the ability to stay relaxed in your daily teaching life. It's obviously impossible to do this at every point of your teaching day, but you can develop some very effective habits that you can call upon at any time and in any place. The ability to get yourself into a calm state and be able to focus your energy productively is something you can learn and become proficient at.

Some people call this meditation, and others call it focused breathing. I call it being within my own stillness. With all the technology and gadgets available today and all the demands that modern Western lifestyles produce, this is the one thing that can literally keep you sane. Call it what you will, but it is the art of being calm and even more importantly being focused (or refocused) that will help you become a more effective teacher. This is a skill like any other, and the more time and awareness you put into practice, the more benefits you will discover.

The most common response I have heard to this idea (and I used to use it myself) is, "Where on God's earth am I ever going to find the time to do this in my teaching day? And where am I ever going to find a quiet place at school?" The simplest thing to do is to sit down and make out a time budget. Look for a time where you could possibly do nothing. The best thing about fitting meditation into your teaching day is that it can fit anywhere and into any amount of time.

Can you spare ten seconds here or there in your day? This is exactly where I started some years back. I would stand (or sometimes sit) in the middle of a crowded preschool classroom, close my eyes, and practice breathing for ten seconds. Sometimes I was feeling stressed, and other times I wasn't. Eventually, I began to encourage my students to do the same. It took a total of ten seconds out of the teaching day. I built this up to thirty seconds over time, and sometimes even up to a minute. This is possible when transitioning students from one lesson to another.

It has become commonplace in all of my classrooms that, when students come in from lunch and playground break times, they sit and breathe. I have trained them to know that the first three minutes is "quiet and breathing" time. This gets them calm and focused and ready to learn for the next session. As all legendary teachers know, you can train your students to follow almost any classroom procedure.

Other places where you could meditate or breathe for yourself might be in a storeroom or spare room somewhere, or even a spare toilet stall. The better you get at training yourself to breath and be calm, the more you will realise that you can do it almost anywhere. Get on the internet and look up different types of meditations and breathing practices. I cannot stress enough how important this is to your health and well-being long-term.

Sure, other teachers may laugh at you or make jokes about you, but it says a whole lot more about them than it does about you. Just watch them get more and more stressed throughout their teaching day. Be proud to be yourself and proud of your proactive decision to lead a healthier and more productive teaching life. This starts with your ability to take in one of the best resources known to teaching, which is completely free of charge at any time of the day: oxygen.

As you will be on your feet a lot as a teacher, you will at some point, regardless of your age and physical ability, get very sore feet. There are several ways to remedy this, and all are highly effective at keeping you in the game and keeping your teaching at optimum performance levels. The first is to get a regular foot massage. Just like a body massage, this is important to your well-being and physical health. Find a good reflexologist—your feet will thank you for it.

Another valuable tool for your feet is a Dr. Graeme massager. Find him online at-www.drgraeme.com, and you will never look back. These are high-strength handheld massagers that are about the size of a large hairdryer. They are the weapon of choice for all good physiotherapists and will work wonders on your tired aching feet (and your neck, shoulders, and back too). If you have a husband, wife, or significant other, persuade them to give your body a blast with one of these. These massagers also have unique pulsating operating feature that can really loosen up your aching body part. Dr. Graeme is a fantastic guy, and he will send one to you anywhere in the world. He is also open to questions and comments about his products and will give discounts for multiple orders. Find him once again at www.drgraeme.com, and tell him that you read it here in my book. He will love you for it.

Another Great product that works well with these hand held massagers is a set of Roll Model-Massage Therapy Balls. These were developed by Jill Miller in the U.S.A. They are a set of soft (but not too hard) yoga balls, which are about the size of a tennis ball. These are however (unlike a tennis ball) designed to mould to you aching body part as you roll on them. Just like the Dr. Graeme massagers you can apply as much or as little pressure as you want. These can work miracles especially in the arches of your feet. Check out her website-www.therollmodel.com for all her fantastic products. And again your body will love you for it.

Alternatively or additionally, you can find yourself a traditional masseur. There are sports, deep tissue, remedial, Thai, trigger point, lymphatic, aroma, and kahuna (with essential oils) massages, just to name a few. I have had all of these at different stages in my teaching life as my needs have changed with my professional journey. The key here is to just go and do it. In a high-pressure, high-stress job like teaching, you want to feel your best as much as physically possible. Don't be one of those teachers who gets a massage every six years when they're on a holiday (vacation). Make it a regular part of your lifestyle. Even a massage once every six weeks to two months is helpful. I guarantee that once you make this a habit, your body will start to tell you when it's time for another one.

As my current (and extremely wonderful) masseur Helen said to me a little while back, "There is nothing wrong with feeling good physically, and this has an enormous effect on your mental well-being also." Remember that a teacher who feels good physically feels better mentally and emotionally and teaches more effectively.

Another physical tool that's a must for any beginning teacher (or any teacher for that matter) is a teaching journal. This can be anything from a small notepad to a bound hardcover book. Go to your local office-supply store and find the one that feels right for you. Not only does a journal allow you to reflect on your teaching life and experiences, but it can become a great personal historical record of your professional life. As an added bonus, it enables you to get difficult things off your chest and onto paper as a form of stress relief. You will be amazed at how useful writing things down can be as you develop better problem-solving skills for yourself.

It's always good to reflect back on your thoughts about different issues you will encounter and how your perceptions change with time. Of course, all these things take time out of your busy day, and with added responsibilities like paying off cars and houses and raising a family, these things are not always possible all the time. If you're only able to write in your teaching journal once every couple of days, then go with it. Even if it's only once a week or once every couple of weeks, so be it. From my own experience, when I first became a teacher, I journaled almost every day. Then, over the years, it has moved to once every school term (usually during a holiday or vacation break).

One of the best things about a teaching journal is that it will become your memory. You will have many weird and wonderful teaching experiences, and as much as you think you can remember them offhand, you won't. You can practice your memory just like a muscle, but this is where your journal comes into play. As soon as you read about your experiences in your journal, it will take you back just like it happened yesterday. Some teaching events will be either so fantastic or traumatic that they will be seared into your memory forever. But it's the little things that you can recall with the use of a journal that will help you gain clarity about where you come from as a teacher and where you want to go.

It's like in business: they say to project backwards from the past to project forwards to the future. A teaching journal will give you that valuable insight into your teaching journey thus far and what new direction you might want to take. If you make it a habit to write in it, you'll stick with it, and if you don't, you won't. Again, this is just something that I have found useful, and I hope that you do too.

After you begin your teaching journal writing process, be sure to get yourself a great teaching mentor. It can be a fellow teacher at your school or someone who teaches somewhere else. Work on developing a great sense of trust with your mentor. Let your mentor be your confidant. Believe me, nothing makes you feel better about any situation or problem than talking to someone else about it— especially when that someone is a person who has been there and can either give you useful advice or just listen.

When I say *mentor*, I mean someone who has a lot more experience than you, not someone who is also starting out like you. And when I say *confidant*, I mean someone you can really talk to, not someone you might just chat with occasionally. As a man, I found this relatively hard to do at the beginning of my teaching life. Men usually just have banter sessions and shoot the breeze, so to speak (or just talk a lot of crap). If you are a new male teacher, be the man who can be brave enough to tell someone else that you don't understand a situation or that you may be having trouble working through some issues. These things will come up many times in your teaching life, and as the old saying goes, "A problem shared is a problem halved."

Please, please, please don't ever stop seeking out new mentors, especially as you gain more experience. Even legendary teachers have them, and in some cases they can even become mentors to other legendary teachers through sharing new ideas and fresh perspectives. This mentoring system can work extremely well for all parties involved. And always go into these situations with an open mind.

Another tool you may want to add to your teaching toolkit is humour. The ability to laugh and to see funny things in your teaching life is a gift to yourself beyond measure. I know that some teachers I have taught with over the years will be scoffing in disgust at this notion, because to them teaching is serious business. It's about education, not fun and games. That's a notion that is toxic to your teaching environment.

Laugh and laugh often, especially in front of your students. Show them that you are actually human and can show a little emotion at times. I'm not saying your classroom should resemble an Abbott and Costello movie all the time, but take time to include humour and light-heartedness into your teaching day. I guarantee you'll once again be surprised by the results.

Introduce joke sessions into your classroom routine and study how your students react. This can be done with students of any age or background. Not only does it teach confidence and good public speaking, but this is a great way for your students to connect with each other. I haven't yet met a person who didn't like to hear a (tasteful and appropriate) joke. This is one habit that is actually good for you and good for others around you. Laughter is the true elixir that bonds us all together in the craziness of the teaching world.

One of the most essential tools you could ever possess as a teacher is a sense of optimism. If you are born with this, that's great, but you can also learn and refine this like any other skill. It can ultimately make or break you as a teacher, as you will encounter the opposite, which is pessimism, a lot in your teaching journey. You will meet teachers who will inspire you with their positivity, and on the flip side, you will meet teachers who seem to drag you down. The key here is to stay positive in your own healthy way. Not to say that you can be optimistic and positive all the time about your teaching. But you can make healthy choices about what type of attitude you adopt each moment of each teaching day and allow this to guide your thoughts.

Some situations will test you and stretch you to your limits. This should be viewed as a positive aspect of teaching. How will you ever know how strong, courageous, or flexible you can be if you are never tested? It would be a bit like buying a new four-wheel drive vehicle and never taking it off-road to see what it's capable of. In some ways, I even advocate putting yourself on the firing line with certain tasks or responsibilities to see what you're really made of. You could do this cautiously at first and just test the proverbial water, or if you're feeling adventurous, you could jump straight in. Like actor Paul Hogan once said in a TV interview, "Bite off more than you can chew, and then chew like crazy."

The best part is, it doesn't really matter what you decide to do, so long as you keep making a conscious effort to do things that mean something to you. If you believe in the meaning, you will always have an inner conviction to follow through with it. This breeds positive energy, as you know that when your heart and soul are into something (especially a teaching project), you won't really care what others think of you. You will either be too absorbed in it or be having too much fun to notice anyone else's negativity.

I would just like to share this little story about how I learnt to deal with negative teachers in my career. I would greet them each and every day by name and smile sincerely when I did this. Then I would send them lots of peace and love for their teaching day. Then surprise, surprise, over a period time, I would watch these people begin to soften. I would even begin to see them smile and say good morning back to me. In some rare cases, they would even say good morning to me first. Then I would casually ask how they were doing and try to get to know them a little. Not that I was wanting to be their friend, but just to share my positivity with them. In nine out of ten cases, I found that their negativity stemmed from some negative lifestyle choices or negative event they had experienced.

Most people are just looking for some gentle encouragement and recognition. You can be the instigator for this. You don't have to own other people's attitudes or problems, but you can own the ability to reach out to others even in a small way by spreading a little bit of optimism and positivity here and there. If you think this is really Pollyanna...ish, you're absolutely correct.

Another great tool for your teaching toolkit is your students' parents. As a teacher of mostly young children, I have had perhaps thousands of interactions with these people in my teaching life. The key word here is not *parents* as such but a word that has become a catchphrase for our modern era: *networking*. Your students' parents are the best source of help and resources you will ever know, especially if you teach in public education. Parents of students have businesses and contacts within the community which are just there waiting for you to incorporate into your classroom.

No matter where you school or learning institution is located, the parents of these young minds you are paid to teach will help you with acquiring anything if only you have the courage to ask for it. And they, in turn, will appreciate being needed—I guarantee it. Yes, everyone like to bang on about how busy they are and how they don't have time to do this or to do that, but it's actually quite simple. Get everyone's email address and just send out a blanket email about what your class is doing and what you may require to make this learning experience more entertaining for your students. You may even attract these parents into your classroom to become helpers. Any legendary teacher I have ever know or even heard of has never refused a parent helper into their classroom on any level.

Now, all the experienced teachers may be out there reading this saying, "I don't want certain parents anywhere near my classroom. They gossip, they interrupt, they show favouritism to their child, etc." Yes, these things may happen, but you can dictate whether they happen or not. State very clearly what help is needed and when. Then be very clear to each visitor to your classroom what your expectations are.

You will certainly get nosy, inconsiderate, irritating parents hanging around on occasions. But just like the students, let everyone know the rules first and how this applies to them. I have seen nosy, inconsiderate, and irritating parents stop being so when they know that you run an open classroom where everyone is welcome and where they know that their child is well cared for and is having fun learning.

I have been blessed with many fantastic parent helpers over the years with a myriad of activities and experiences. Some of these people have become my lifelong friends, and I have shared the fantastic experience of watching their children grow into responsible, well-balanced individuals. You too can create this welcoming environment within your classroom, which in turn can help you build a greater sense of worth for your school, college, university, and community.

Now, if you want to take the "I just don't have time" road, that's fine. Your efforts will reap whatever it is that you put out there in the universe. I have also been guilty of not employing this tactic on rare occasions, and what I got back was suspicion and negativity. This taught me many valuable lessons on community engagement and how I fit into my community as a servant to my students' educational needs. The key to promoting this greater sense of community is to think beyond your own selfish needs as a teacher and get your students involved in projects that put their focus beyond themselves. Nothing makes students of any age feel more alive than being actively engaged in something that helps someone else or benefits others in a greater sense.

Just a final note about staying positive: when you have to teach at close range with an individual or group that is extremely or even mildly negative, you could try Wayne Dyer's approach of sending them peace and love each time you see or think of them. Always greet them with a smile (even a forced one) and pay them a small compliment. Always say something positive about their teaching, or even give them a small gift like a box of chocolates occasionally for no particular reason. This will compound your role as a positive teaching force in the universe and will even soften them up to reveal quite often a positive individual within that had just forgotten how to be positive.

I have actually taken the step of seeing it as my life's mission to attract these people just to allow them to see love, kindness, goodness, and of course positivity in every aspect of their lives, not just their teaching. Take the challenge as you will, and approach this any way you like. The best part about it is that positivity is highly infectious. Get to it.

Another important tool that is a must for your teaching toolkit is the art of giving compliments. Sure, we need to be lavish with our praise for our students, but this must also be spread liberally with your teaching colleagues. Think about the last time you got some praise or a positive compliment from a workmate in your teaching life. The answer is probably never, or so long ago that you just can't remember, right? Be the leader in the field of spreading positive vibes throughout your school, and even go so far as to look for opportunities to give lavish praise to all you come into contact with.

Some people may be taken aback at first, and their low self-esteem may push it off as purely superficial. But with practice and persistence, you can change people's attitudes towards themselves and their teaching by simply putting good, honest, decent compliments out there for them to enjoy. At first, some of your colleagues may think it is some kind of practical joke. But with a little bit of creativity and perseverance, this can truly work miracles.

How do I know this? I actually do this all the time and in many types of unexpected ways. One way that I really go all out to help people feel appreciated for their efforts is to give random gifts or compliments to various staff members at random times of the year. In my years of teaching, I have always loved and respected my teacher aides, and I make a point of singling one of them out for a special treat every so often. This also goes for our school librarian, our technical support officer, our head of curriculum, and the most important person, our office manager. These people go above and beyond to make my life as a teacher more organised and much more rewarding with help and a truckload of access to educational resources and new ideas. Without them, my teaching life would be a lot harder.

I challenge you to find someone in your school worthy of praise and high esteem. It could be a teacher or someone in a supporting role. Make it a habit to spread the love, and it will come back to you tenfold. It creates a very different dynamic to work in, especially in high-pressure and high-stress places like a school. The best thing is that it tells everyone around you that they are not alone. Your team is with you all the way, and you can always achieve more together.

CHAPTER 6

TAKE A BREAK

TAKING BREAKS IN your teaching day allows you and your students to survive to see the end of it. Dale Carnegie, in his famous book *Stop Worrying and Start Living*, describes a very unique situation where some steelworkers participated in an experiment of resting several times each hour on the job to increase productivity. The aim was to get them to rest at set times and regularly enough to ensure they did not suffer from fatigue. This experiment proved highly successful; with all of these extra short breaks, they managed to increase productivity. Carnegie went on to point out that the US Army has also adopted this practice, allowing infantry soldiers to drop their packs on long marches for ten minutes every hour to keep them going.

Prominent people throughout the twentieth century, like Winston Churchill, John D. Rockefeller, and Eleanor Roosevelt, took a specific time each day to have breaks and rest. Carnegie also suggests that one take a break before one gets tired to ensure that the onset of fatigue does not force one to stop. As teachers, we are at the forefront of our students' production of thoughts and beliefs, and this would serve us well also.

Another important element in your teaching journey is longevity. Remember that teaching is a marathon and not a sprint. You want be there at the end, looking back at your teaching journey with fondness and celebrating good memories and pleasant learning experiences. Focus on these positive points and not the carnage and chaos that generally represent an average day-to-day teaching experience.

The first type of break is the fruit-snack break or healthy-snack break. This involves the students (and teachers) all bringing in a piece of fresh fruit or vegetable of some kind. This break only needs to last for a few minutes, and to save time and mess, the fruit or vegetable can be brought into the classroom already cut up and prepared in a small washable container. This can teach your students important lessons on how to not only eat healthy food but also be conscious of packaging and waste that can end up in a landfill or in our oceans. Garden compost bins can be set up to receive any excess fruit or vegetables peels or scraps. This can also inspire a classroom or school garden program.

Another benefit of having this break is to allow students (and again teachers) to eat something between breakfast and lunch. They can give your blood sugar level a little boost to get everyone through the first session of the school day.

Another type of break is a talking break. This one is particularly popular with primary (elementary) students. It can last anywhere from one to five minutes, depending on how long your lessons go for. It can take place every thirty minutes or so to give your students a chance to stand up, stretch their legs for a couple of minutes, and have a quick chat with their friends.

It may be a good idea to set up some rules for this type of break to ensure that you don't get any unruly or inappropriate behaviour, such as loud conversation, wrestling, or running around the classroom. Any students who break these rules can be sent back their desks immediately or sent to a designated time-out area. I have yet to meet a student who doesn't want to have an opportunity to chat with friends during class time.

Another break is the joke break or joke-time break. All this involves is for you to choose two or three students to come up in front of the class and tell an appropriate joke. Encourage your students to find new jokes in books or on the internet to tell to the class. This once again gives students a little time between lessons or sessions to relax and get their focus back. This is also a great way to develop and enhance your students' social skills. One of the best sounds I have ever had the privilege of hearing is the sound of young children's genuine laughter. Your students will get a real kick out of seeing you laugh too.

Another break is the game break. This can be in the form of an organised crowd game within the classroom, generally at the end of a lesson or session. It gives students a goal to aim for through reinforcing positive behaviour and also enhances and develops their valuable social skills. Games are fun, and when I was a young child, I loved having fun at school with my friends (as all children do).

If for any reason certain students do not comply with appropriate behaviours, they can be excluded from the activity and once again sent to a time-out area. They'll soon work out that it's much better to behave and be part of the fun than to miss out.

Another break is the jogging break or running break. This is where you take a few minutes in between lessons to allow your students to jog or run around a designated path, oval, or playground. If that is not possible, you can have them follow a simple obstacle course set up around the classroom or basketball court that incorporates as many different physical movements or exercises as possible. Ask your students for ideas on this and get them to draw up a detailed map incorporating resources that are easily obtainable. Nothing is impossible if you open your mind to different ideas and creative thinking. This can also be incorporated into a short Yoga break also. Learn some simple Yoga moves that can be done in a small or confined space. This can also allow students to give their body a simple stretch and give them time to give their mind a short break too.

Another break is the meditation break or relaxing break. This one comes in very handy when students come back all energetic from lunchtime and afternoon tea play time. Students either sit at their desks or find a free space on the floor. Set some rules with this that involve students not talking or being silly with each other. Turn off the classroom lights and turn on a small lamp or some rechargeable candles as a physical symbol that the silent break has begun.

Teach students a simple breathing technique that allows their body to absorb as much oxygen as possible. Train them to take a deep breath through their nose and to suck the incoming air right down into the pit of their stomach. I tell my students to blow their tummy up like it's a balloon. Then I get them to imagine the remaining air filling up their lungs. Then I get them to hold their breath in for two to three seconds and then to let the air out very slowly through their mouth, as if they are blowing through a straw. They can keep their eyes open, but as a general rule for being relaxed, it would be preferable that their eyes remain closed for the entire time.

This break only needs to go for anywhere from three to five minutes depending on the students' mood. Get on the internet and check out other breathing techniques to teach to your students. I can guarantee that you will soon find a noticeable difference in their concentration skills and their personal insight into their own learning.

One of the most important breaks you can ever have in your class, especially if you are teaching young children, is a play break. This could involve anything and everything that involves appropriate play for the student's age group. Many governments and academics dismiss play as being a waste of good learning time, but in fact, as a preschool teacher, I found that play was the most essential element for teaching young children how to interact with and find their place in the world. The social and emotional aspects of play for young children—or in fact for just about anybody at any age group—is invaluable.

It continually baffles me how, in Australia, the government has all but abolished play-based learning in prep years and preschools. Children are expected to begin to read at four years of age. Yes, it is possible to teach a child of any age to read, yet how they interact socially with their surroundings will have, in my opinion, a bigger impact on their health and well-being in later years. We are not allowing our students to play anywhere near as much as they used to. And somewhere along the line, we are expecting them to step up academically.

So I pose this question: Are our students feeling more socially adjusted? Are the rates of teenage suicide dropping? Are the rates of prescription medications for our children also dropping? Are our younger generations optimistic about their future? I'm not sure they are. Children today in Australia and in most First World Westernised countries seem to be behind the eight ball all the time. It seems to me as a teacher that they are unable to enjoy their younger years and just be children.

Yes, times change, and generations change, and economics brings change, and all that. But our children today are no different from the children of yesterday. They are no different from the children twenty or thirty years ago. They still need nurturing and guidance and love in a way that works. As a teacher I believe in play breaks because they allow students of all ages to see their world through unstructured eyes. It's these unstructured ways of seeing things that can allow them to really find their own way to learning. This can happen through experimentation and exploration, not through clinical instruction.

Play breaks can be from five to twenty minutes or as long as you wish. These breaks can involve your students accessing a range of activities with which they can engage or disengage at any time. Breaks can take the form of dress-up areas, puzzle tables, science tables, water-play areas, construction areas, and so on. Pretty much any type of play area can be incorporated into your classroom if you really want it to.

Having enough space can be an obstacle, but you can easily rotate resources and activities at different times throughout the school year to incorporate everything. You can experiment with different types of play resources to maximise the interaction with your students. The best part is that you as the teacher can just keep reinventing the activities for whatever age group you are teaching.

Some older students may find it strange to adjust to a play break, but with constant positive reinforcement, it can become a normal part of your classroom routine. Try it and watch what a huge difference it will make to your student's behaviour levels and social interaction skills. As Albert Einstein once famously stated, "Creativity is more important than facts." Please ponder this for a while.

Don't forget to take a break for yourself on occasion. A teacher's life can be stressful and overwhelming at times, and this is when personal breaks become a must. You can benefit greatly from this practice. Find a storeroom or a quiet area somewhere in your classroom or building and just close your eyes and breathe. It really is that simple. Do this each day for a couple of minutes when your students are having their lunch break. If you can't do it every day, schedule it for a couple of times a week. Do it for a minute if you think you can't spare two.

I can guarantee you one thing with these very important personal breaks: the more you include them in your daily school routine, the more you will look forward to them, and the more frequent and longer they will magically become. Make it work for you.

For personal breaks away from your educational life, take a weeknight off each week and do absolutely nothing. Go for a walk by yourself and just have "you" time. If you are married and have a family, structure this into your weekly routine. Once again, if you believe it can be done, it will get done; and if you believe it can't, it won't. The success of this simple act of alone time is entirely up to you. Make it a priority, and it will allow you to have time when you can gain valuable insight into yourself.

All legendary teachers know the value of personal insight and how to use this in their classroom. Being emotionally balanced within yourself is a key ingredient to a long and healthy teaching life.

You need time to step back from the chaos (if only momentarily) and gain some clarity. This, along with regular meditation, is a crucial part of knowing yourself and knowing what's important to you in your teaching life.

Another break that is essential to your emotional balance is to plan different things for your holiday (vacation) breaks. Make plans to travel or to have an adventure of some kind for each holiday as it comes up. You could even plan your whole year's holidays in advance. Include activities that you haven't done before, or even plan some travel to places you've never been before. These ideas will give you what many call *childhood wonder*. This is the wonder we all had as children about how we discover new things in our world.

The strange thing is that as adults, we have more resources than ever to really get into this, and somehow we seem to forget about it. Make a conscious effort to get it back and make it a priority in your life. If you have financial commitments, such a mortgage or young children, you will have fewer options, of course. Get your positivity into gear and create less-expensive options. Brainstorm this with your partner or friends, and think about what it is you really want to explore in these holiday times.

Talk to others about their travel experiences, and you'll be amazed at what you can learn. I have never met people who don't love to tell others about their travel adventures. In fact, I sincerely believe that most of our travel adventures happen purely so we can share them with each other. And teachers are notorious travellers and adventurers.

All legendary teachers know the value of stepping away from the humdrum of your daily routine to really get your thoughts and creative juices flowing again. Be brave, and like the Nike ads have been telling us all these years: "Just do it."

CHAPTER 7

DO LESS, AND DO
IT BETTER

THE GREATEST IRONY in this whole book is how I lay out all these great ideas and procedures for you to follow and then boldly proclaim that you don't really need to do any of them by doing less and doing it better. That may be a contradiction, but it's a good contradiction, because it basically says that you can do all of these things or none of these things and still be productive. The teaching profession is full of ironies and contradictions about everything. The government will instil policies within education that contradict each other. Admins will tell you one thing and then turn around and tell you something else. Parents will give you contradictory messages about their children. Even your teaching colleagues will give your contradictory messages about what's in and what isn't.

To discern what is important to you and how you can apply it effectively is the key to gaining a greater understanding of how you can actually achieve more in a teaching day by doing less. The greatest irony that all legendary teachers already know is that the more teaching work you do at school, the more you will find to do, and the more you will realise that it never really all gets done. Being the busiest teacher is not a goal you ever want to attain. It's right up there with being the most stressed-out teacher. Work smarter, not harder.

The strangest thing about living in this First World Westernised culture is how everyone is always going on about how busy they are. We are constantly telling ourselves that we are busy doing this and busy doing that. Yes, we can be busy doing things or at least getting things done, and this is important to a certain degree. But most people associate being busy with being important.

Dale Carnegie, in his famous book *How to Win Friends and Influence People*, describes at great length how every individual on this planet yearns for a feeling of importance. And perhaps to a lesser degree, we also crave a feeling of appreciation or maybe even admiration. Somehow, I feel that this sense of importance has been caught up with being busy for the fact that it's meant to make you feel like you are achieving something more. Busy people are getting things done, therefore they are perceived or at least perceive themselves as being successful.

We tend to relate success in our modern culture with achievement and achievement with fulfilment, which is meant to bring happiness. Our culture tends to bang on about how happy we should all be and what happiness is meant to be. I could really go to town about the advertising industry here and how everything they are trying to sell you will bring you happiness, or at least help you in your busy life to be happier. But when all is said and done, any sense of importance, fulfilment, and happiness comes from within ourselves and from our perceptions of ourselves.

The great Wayne Dyer has described this many times in his talks about how we are not human doings but human beings. So why do we still crave this sense of doing things all the time and being busy? Being busy in my perception is more about making choices that can enhance your life and ultimately enhance your well-being.

I believe that this feeling of being busy also stems from a sense of low self-esteem that comes from fear of being bored—or perhaps even fear of having any still moments in your life where you may be required to deal with yourself. This is not to say that all busy people have low self-esteem, but it is interesting how being busy can inhibit your ability to undertake proper self-care. This can include being too busy to eat healthily or being too busy to exercise or even too busy to stop being busy and to rest.

These busy lives can unfortunately be coped with in our culture by excessive consumption of alcohol, drugs (both prescription and illegal), caffeine, fast foods, and energy drinks. Like everything else in your life, these are choices you make on a daily basis. If you want to make excuses, that is also a very important choice that you are making. Get a copy of Wayne Dyer's *Excuses Begone* and make some serious choices about your health and your future, which includes not being busy for the sake of trying to look important or even happy.

Getting back to being busy as a teacher: yes, by the nature of the work we do, teachers are naturally busy people. But even as teachers, we need to let go of this notion of being busy, because this is one the main causers of stress, and not the good kind either. This negative stress, as you may be aware, is not something you want in your life either on a permanent or semi-permanent basis. Getting things done as a teacher is not a competition with other teachers about who is achieving the most, either.

Busy teachers are not necessarily productive teachers. At times in my teaching, I have associated being busy with being useful. I have led myself down the path of burnout many times under the guise of being useful. Yes, being useful is helpful in working as a team, and this is essential to how a great school operates. But taking this to the extreme where you are seeking the approval of others is not a place you want to be, either physically or emotionally.

Through personal insight and perhaps even a spiritual path in your personal life, you can find a good balance for really being yourself in your professional life. This is what the great Abraham Maslow described as being a self-actualised person. This is basically where you do what you love and love what you do. When you take time to reflect on what's really important in your life at various stages, the things that will be memorable will not be the times of busyness and stress, I can guarantee you. Be a giving teacher, sure, but make sure that in the giving, you save some time for yourself and for what's really important to you and those close to you.

Work out how you can actually do less and do it better. This can be done, and if you are to survive as a teacher long-term, I would even suggest that it must be done. Take time out for yourself. This may be relatively easy if you are single, but not so much if you are married and especially if you have children. Once again, it's all about making choices and prioritising things properly. Go on date nights with your partner. Learn yoga or meditation in order to be able to truly relax and regain your focus. This will bring you back in touch with yourself and give you a greater sense of your own power, especially when it comes to making decisions about how and when to use it. Remember that you as a teacher are not a victim of circumstance. You are a wonderful person engaged in one of the most important professions in the world, shaping the next generation and creating a new school of thought.

Another thing that may help you to gain clarity about who you are as a teacher and as a learner is to create a sea change (or tree change) for yourself. As a teacher, you are blessed by the fact that just like doctors and chefs, you can work just about anywhere on this glorious earth. The world really is your oyster. Pick a spot on the map and make a decision to take steps to go there to work as a teacher. The internet is teaming with teaching jobs everywhere, and there is always one that is just right for you.

Please don't misunderstand my intentions: I am not encouraging you to go off blindly and throw away all of your responsibilities. But rather, when the time is right for you. Go where you feel you are called to be. You need to grow and develop as a teacher and as a person, and this will involve teaching in some jobs and places that you have not yet imagined. But strangely enough, it's these places that teach you the most about who you are as a teacher and what levels of personal insight you can gain. And as Helen Keller famously stated that "life is either a daring adventure or it is nothing at all."

I encourage you to take a leap of faith into the adventure zone of teaching and see where it takes you. Nothing ventured, nothing gained. Trust that a power greater than yourself is looking out for you always.

When you actually push yourself beyond what you consider normal or even safe, you will be amazed by the results. Things may not go smoothly. You may not come into fame and fortune (at least not straight away). But remember: teaching is always about helping others achieve to their fullest potential and leaving a legacy of your own passions and values for the next generation to build on. I feel the best thing about even writing this is that I can feel myself being inspired by my own words. I think back to some of the places I've lived and taught in, and it motivates me to push on to greater heights as a teacher. That and the fact that in writing this book, I might even inspire someone like you.

Another insight I would like to share with you as a teacher is that the world is not riding on your shoulders. Teachers have this strange perception that if they are not there to do everything and to handle everything, then the world (and their classroom) will fall into a heap. Absolute nonsense! Yes, you need to take responsibility for your job as a teacher and follow the appropriate protocols, but there is no reward for playing the martyr. In fact, if you do, you will only short-change yourself and alienate everyone around you. You are always going to be part of a team, and the team does need you, but there should be a healthy balance of give and take. Your relationship with your school, classroom, and greater organisation depends on you only as much as you need it to.

If you find yourself wanting to impress everybody by taking on too much, step back and ease off a little. Delegate where necessary and learn the value of saying no to tasks that are either beyond you or are stretching you too thin. You have to know yourself well enough to know where the burnout line is. Sometimes you will learn this the hard way, as you may need to, and sometimes it will be obvious to you.

Burnt-out teachers are no good to anybody. Work to your strengths, become more aware of your weaknesses, and find the balance that is right for you. You will find that balance when you are happy to go to school each day and know that you are making a worthy contribution to your students and their lives.

I recall a study that I read about many years ago where an author interviewed a thousand business executives who were at the end of their lives—some even on their deathbeds. The common theme that the author found most striking when reflecting on their lives was that not one of these individuals said they wished they had spent more time at the office. The same is true for me when asking many soon-to-be-retired teachers. Not one of them said they wished they had spent more time at school trying to stay busy. Yes, we spend a lot of time at school working at and preparing our teaching lives but we do need a good sense of balance with as with everything in life. Food for thought.

Experience will teach you many things. Get in touch with your beliefs and values and work those into what makes you passionate. There are a myriad of teaching jobs out there that you can undertake. Believe in yourself enough to know that there is always something you can contribute to a classroom, school, college, university, or the profession itself. It's about being open to what's possible and how your own ideas can be entwined into this. And again as Gary Zukav states in his amazing book *The heart of the soul*, "If you first believe it, then you'll see it."

A very important part of doing less and doing it better is to learn to filter what will work for you and your classroom and what won't. The most bizarre thing about our modern education system as we know it is that there always seems to be someone somewhere trying to tell us that there is some way of doing something better. Sure, as teachers and educators, we should be striving to improve ourselves and continually developing and acquiring new skills, but somehow

I feel this has gone into overkill. Our politicians and educational leaders seem to think that we, the teachers, are lacking in every skill, as we seem to be on this never-ending path of in-servicing and upskilling to the point of it becoming ridiculous. I can feel thousands of teachers worldwide nodding their heads in agreement.

Every government seems to think it has the magic bullet to fix every problem that ever existed in our schools. They promise to weed out "lazy teachers" and to fix the curriculum once and for all. As with any intention, this may have a noble beginning, but the results are far from perfect. In fact, the result of all of these necessary changes is overloading teachers with new ideas to saturation point.

I have sat through many presentations, forums, and conferences where everything relayed is a must-have in the classroom. The only result of this is teachers with glazed eyes and folded arms. They are tired of fix-it solutions and a business-like approach to education. Education is about introducing ideas and creating environments where students can work with those ideas. It's not about trying to produce something tangible and measurable for the sake of educational chest-beating or trying to keep up with best school results.

In my experience, students learn better when there is no pressure to perform. It's great to want to do well academically, but not at the expense of one's well-being or livelihood. It's like our educational system is wanting us, the teachers, to prepare students to face a dog-eat-dog world, to aim for the top no matter what, and to walk all over anyone who may get in your way. This teaches our students nothing but fear that there are limited resources in the world, and that they'd better get in first. What we need to teach our students instead is that our world is a place of trust and faith. Everything else flows from and through this.

This may sound like New Age rubbish, but I have taught this to many of my students, and many years later, as they are all graduating from high school, I am seeing some fantastic results. Believing in this makes me believe in myself also. I have witnessed this having a huge flow-on effect for not only my students but also their siblings, parents, families, and the greater community. School should be a place where everyone can find a niche and be happy within it—where confidence and self-appreciation are not only valued but cherished.

It's also important to view your teaching load like a metaphorical wagon—the old horse-and-buggy type from early last century. Your teaching wagon can only take on so much stuff. When the wagon is full, then you can't physically or emotionally take on any more.

At a staff meeting a few years back, our principal put up a photo from the internet of a donkey suspended in mid-air whilst still harnessed to a cart unbelievably overloaded with bales of cotton. All the teachers laughed at how ridiculous this looked. The principal obviously wanted to illustrate that being overloaded in any capacity was completely unproductive. The sad thing was that about six months later, I tried to explain to the same principal that this picture of the donkey was now my teaching reality, and that I wasn't laughing anymore. Needless to say, I left the school the next year (and he left the year after that).

When your teaching wagon is overloaded, you are going nowhere fast. But even if you could (as most admins will make you believe) take on that little bit extra, something will have to fall off the other side if you are to keep your feet on the ground and keep moving forward. As I have come to realise over the years, the best way to enjoy and thrive in your teaching life is to always have a little space on your wagon for anything special or interesting that may come along. This, my friends, is the true art of legendary teaching: to be able to keep this juggling act in perfect balance.

How do you manage this? The first step is to do what's acceptable to you as far as your workload goes. You need to set very clear boundaries about what you are prepared to do and what you are not. This presents a mental dilemma for beginning teachers, as they will do almost everything they are told just to keep their job. This can be a good thing and a bad thing.

Many years ago, when I somehow by default (and believe me, it was like that) found myself working as a teaching director of a day-care centre, I barely had two years of preschool teaching under my belt when I was thrown into the chaotic world of administration. If I had my time over, I would have really said no to this with gusto, but for all its intensity, this role did actually teach me some valuable lessons that I have always been grateful for. The one thing I remember most was that I treated my staff (some of whom were beginning teachers like me) as equals. I asked for their opinions on everything, and I respected what they had to say about the important day-to-day issues. I treated my experienced teachers with the respect that they deserved, and this paid back many dividends, which I was always grateful for.

The point I'm trying to make here is that you will know whether or not you are working for an understanding admin. If you are, that's great. If you suspect you aren't, you may need to make some decisions about whether you want to stay in that particular job long-term. When you take charge of decisions like this, you take back the power over how much of a teaching workload you are prepared to take on. That decision is entirely up to you.

If you are constrained by having a mortgage or are bringing up a young family or whatever, you have fewer options, but you still have options. No one can make you stay in a teaching situation that is not conducive to your overall well-being and happiness. If you have to step back a little and teach part-time, then so be it. If you need to look around for other teaching opportunities, then do it, even if they pay less. Make any necessary changes in your teaching life that you need to. Design your life around your immediate future, and work your finances into this the best way you can.

Ask yourself some serious questions about your lifestyle and how you can survive with modified resources. I'm not suggesting that you go without anything, but what is it that you really need, and what is in your life that is just a luxury you could do without? Having fewer things (possessions) in your life doesn't make you less of a person. If you are chasing status and recognition through the car you drive or the house you live in, then I would ask you, is this the way you wish to conduct your life as a teacher long-term?

I spent last year clearing out my house of all the clutter I had acquired over the years. I cleared out clothes, sports gear, shoes, furniture, and a host of other stuff I thought I needed and couldn't do without. The biggest thing I cleared out was old teaching resources. As a teacher, you will acquire a lot of resources as you progress through your years of teaching. The best thing to do is keep giving away what you haven't used in, say, two or three years. Pass them on to someone else, and the abundant universe once again will pay you back in multiples.

Another aspect of doing less and doing it better is teacher coaching. In all my years of being coached, I think the only thing I ever learnt from this (or perhaps more felt) was that I was incompetent, possibly broken, and needed to be fixed. I would go so far as to say that I feel that coaching in the field of education has been a total waste of time and money on an industrial scale. Yet the government in all its wisdom seems to think this is a good idea and should continue at all costs. As much as this sounds extremely negative and doesn't paint a good picture for those doing the coaching, I have found that in many cases, I actually knew a lot more than the coach did—to the point where things bordered on outright embarrassment.

I recall several years ago being informed that I was to be coached on how to teach preschool more effectively. We were apparently going to be taught how to "do it better." At first, I was excited and eager to get into some new ideas and concepts. Then I was introduced to my coach. Now, being a very perceptive person, I soon realised that something didn't seem right. My coach seemed to be saying all the right things to me (and the other teachers), but something didn't quite add up. I must stress that being around young children for many years has taught me the value of detecting non-truths at twenty paces, especially when coming out of the mouth of an adult.

I thought I would take it upon myself to investigate this a little bit further and ask questions about the coach's experience in preschool or even early childhood teaching. The reply was that this individual had never taught any primary or early childhood grades; the coach's background was high school English. Well, as you can imagine, this sent alarm bells ringing in my head and prompted me to further question my coach's intention for what we had to learn. After that, let's just say that as much as I was just going with my intuition and gut feeling, I instantly earned a reputation for being dissent-ful and disrespectful of my superiors (that is, the coach). After copping a dressing down from my real superiors, the admin, I politely informed them that I had no intention of offending anyone. But however, would never begin to claim myself to be an expert and think that I could then coach a cohort of high school English teachers about how to do their jobs more effectively. Especially when I was a preschool teacher.

After that, I can gladly say that my role at that institution of highly tuned teaching and learning ended soon after—and so did the coach's. But there is a happy ending to this story, and that is that as much as I'm not a fan of teacher coaching, I am a huge fan of teacher mentoring. With mentoring, you are given the opportunity to observe other teachers in action, doing what they love, talking the talk, and walking the walk. You are free to take in anything and everything about what it is they are doing. The best part is that you can, as Al-anon so eloquently puts it, "take what you want and leave the rest."

I have spoken to many teachers about this issue over the years, and I can't say that I've ever seen a single teacher get excited when the word *coaching* was mentioned. But I'm sure that governments and hierarchies will continue to promote this concept in the notion that it sounds catchy and cool and makes them feel like they have invented something new. Good luck to them.

When you are given an opportunity to observe another teacher, you instantly will know what if anything you wish to take from this experience. The best thing for me has been that of all the teacher mentors I've ever observed, I was never once bored or uninterested during these experiences. I always came away with lots of fantastic ideas and concepts that I was able to adapt and implement into my own teaching.

As Gabrielle Bernstein points out in her wonderful book *The Universe Has Your Back*, your working day with your teaching, as with any day in your life, shouldn't be unbelievably difficult. Success with teaching does come through hard work, but it doesn't come through pushing yourself beyond your limits or trying to prove yourself in some way. Yes, teaching can have it difficult moments, but that is all they are: just moments.

Teaching can push you to the brink and make you second-guess yourself, but those are just your perceptions of the situation at a given point in time. Finding your zone and working within that is the key to longevity as a teacher. Being able to constantly step back from what you're doing and keep an objective reflection of yourself can take you to a very different place in your thinking. This once again seems very airy-fairy, and I can imagine many teachers out there thinking, *Man, this wouldn't work with my class* or *Have you ever seen the kids I have to deal with on a day-to-day basis?* But I suggest you look beyond what you immediately see and challenge what it is you think is limiting you as a teacher. Go beyond the story you've told yourself about where you are and where you wish you were heading. Go beyond what the conventions of being ordinary are telling you about your teaching situation.

Remember, there are no mistakes. God and the universe have placed you wherever you are to learn the teaching lessons you need to learn. If you feel that the situation is beyond you, then either take constructive steps to change it or at least change your perceptions of it.

Begin to see the learning that must take place within you as a teacher, and then see the value in this to be able to truly appreciate its gifts. The best part is to have fun with it. Make a game of it with yourself. Throw little challenges in front of yourself to keep things interesting. Look for small ways in which you can make improvements in every aspect of your teaching. Open this whole mindset up to your students and ask for their opinions. Set classroom tasks that carry this common theme and see where they go. As Mahatma Gandhi once famously suggested, "Be the change you want to see in the world."

There is also a thing in our busy teaching lives called *stress*. The mere word conjures up images of people losing control and not being able to function properly, either in their jobs or in life. Stress in your teaching life can become a negative thing when it impacts upon your health and well-being. But please be aware that there is *good* stress out there also. This good stress is something that can be used positively in your day-to-day teaching life. A good stressor could be walking or riding a bicycle to your school. Another could be stepping out of your comfort zone and learning new things. Another could be learning to adapt to difficult situations with the people you encounter each day, such as colleagues, students, and parents. More on this later.

One thing legendary teachers don't do is waste time doing not-so-important things in their teaching life. In our modern world, most people tell themselves that they are too busy to exercise. They are too busy to go to the doctor. They are too busy to begin that book they always wanted to write. I actually used to use that last one quite a bit once upon a time. And the classic: they are too busy to follow their passion in life. The fact is that as teachers, we can waste a lot of time checking emails, checking our phones, surfing the internet, and watching TV. You may claim that all of these things are important to your well-being as a teacher, but they are not.

A legendary teacher knows the value of a good face-to-face conversation with other staff members or students during break times. A legendary teacher knows the value of sitting in a café and people-watching. A legendary teacher knows the value of seeing nature as a good part of unwinding after a day of teaching. My favourite thing to do at the end of most of my teaching days is to ride my bicycle down to the local creek and stick my feet in the water for about ten minutes or so, enjoying the beautiful surrounding rainforest also. Yes, I am unbelievably blessed to be able to do this I know. But find your own little piece of tranquillity and make it work for you. It could be a park or playground or even if you are in a big city, a small patch of grass or even a small area with some indoor plants. Once again it is in your state of mind that dictates how relaxed you can feel and nature (even a small part of it) can help you with this.

A legendary teacher also knows the value of not having to check email every five minutes. Check it once in the morning and once in the evening, and then leave it. Remember the days when you could actually get back to people a few days later and it was okay? Wow.

A legendary teacher knows the value of not being part of social media. Yes, I am on Facebook just like everyone else in the known universe (only for literary purposes, of course), but I have never tweeted or shared any crazy photos with complete strangers on the internet. I see this as a big part of teachers not feeling complete as people. If you feel complete as a person, you don't need to use every social media site going to convince everyone else of this.

I hear you all say, *How can you keep up-to-date with things? How can you reach out to other people? How can you even survive in this modern age without doing any of this?* The simple answer is, because I make a conscious effort to. I decide how I am going to use my time both inside and outside of my teaching life. I decide exactly how busy it is that I want to be both as a teacher and as a person. I decide how to prioritise my time to best suit my needs in every aspect of my teaching and life.

Yes, I get called a technophobe a lot. I get told to move with the times a lot. I get very strange looks from other teachers when I tell them I have never tweeted anything in my life. But I comfort myself in the knowledge that the book I started to write—the one you're reading now—got written because I didn't do these things.

I can tell you that the students I have taught in years gone by still greet me with a gigantic hug and smile because I took the time to listen to them, to get to know them, and to share the best of my teaching self with them because of this. I can tell you that the students I am currently teaching love being in my classes because my mind if not clouded by technology or social media. I love to tell my students first account stories about my life and how they might benefit from this.

I can tell you that the teaching world that I live in has me even inspiring myself—because I can. I give myself permission to be inspired. I give myself permission to be myself, both as a person and as a teacher. And the best part about all of this is that it makes me feel good. And when I feel good I know that I am teaching to my highest potential.

I do know that the mental health units of our hospitals are not getting any smaller. I know that our addictions and compulsions are not going away anytime soon. But I do invite you to ponder on these words for yourself and decide what's important for you. Once again make a game of it, and I guarantee you will be surprised by the results.

Take time out of your busy teaching schedule to smell the proverbial roses. Do things because you want to do them and not just because everyone else is doing it. Be the master of your little teaching universe and give yourself permission to be proud of your own achievements. Be your own greatest fan of your teaching, and once again, you'll be surprised at how many other fans you'll accumulate along the way.

CHAPTER 8
GET INVOLVED

A S MUCH AS the last chapter was about doing less, this chapter encourages you to do more. And not more as in, "Yes, you have to play the martyr and burn out." Doing more in this case means to get involved in your community and incorporate this into your day-to-day classroom activities. Invite the community into your school or even into your classroom. This can be done through special events like fêtes, festivals, fairs, and the like.

Hold special days that revolve around the people you meet. You could celebrate with your students with the traditional mother's and father's day, of course, or you could go further with things like grandparents day or even sibling day, for example. The best part about getting involved and becoming a key member of your community is that you open yourself up to a world of help and support. And of course, there is also the added benefit of networking.

As a teacher of young children, I have never had to stray too far in any direction within the communities I have taught in, either to get help with projects or camps or even get much-needed resources. Once again, it's about being part of something bigger than yourself.

Now you might be reading this and thinking that this is not quite gelling with your personality type. You couldn't imagine doing anything like this or even wanting to. I'm calling for you to be brave and move out of your comfort zone. Do something different to what you have always done. Learn something new about your school or community that you know absolutely nothing about. The benefits of this will amaze you.

This chapter is not about charging off to find your cause and work it to death. It's about making gentle enquiries as to what it is your school or community needs and going with that. There may already be a whole heap of events scheduled, and all you have to do is join in. But don't be afraid to break new ground with this in whatever way you feel could use your expertise. Be a leader your students would be proud to look up to. Be the one who can be creative with new and existing ideas to create a great sense of community or even enhance the existing one. The only limits are the ones you place upon yourself.

The main emphasis here is to be aware of the fact that as a teacher, you by nature are a giver. You should be able to give to your classroom or school as much as you feel comfortable with. There should be no must-dos or guilt trips to make you do anything extra. If there are, either make a decision to stand your ground or make arrangements to seek employment elsewhere.

Remember that as a teacher, your main role is to empower your students, and in doing this, you can also empower yourself. The Bible states, "Remember this, whoever sows sparingly will reap sparingly and whoever sows generously will reap generously. Each person should give what they have decided in their heart to give, not reluctantly or under compulsion, for God loves a cheerful giver" (2 Corinthians 9:6 NIV). So give what you can and let the rest work itself out. Find your niche and work to your strengths with it.

You may wish to push your own boundaries, but don't ever feel compelled to do something that doesn't fit your style or goes against something you truly believe in. Most schools I have found are more than happy for you to give in ways that are acceptable to you. I have learned the hard way over many years as a teacher that the more you give of yourself to causes greater than yourself, the more rewards you will receive in return. This is done humbly and graciously also.

This is not a popularity contest to see who can outdo who; you should all work together as a team (including your students) so that everybody wins. I know this all sounds very utopian and idealistic, but it does actually work when we all chip in and do our bit. Your students will love you for it. They will catch your enthusiasm and run with it, I can guarantee it. In this book, I have guaranteed a lot of positive outcomes, but I have lived and breathed this success with students, parents, and other teachers countless times over the years, and it can work for you too.

When you progress in your teaching career and rise to become a senior teacher, you will be expected to step up and take on more leadership. This is rewarded with more pay, of course, but the added benefit of teaching experience is in knowing where your strengths and weaknesses are. If you take a proactive approach to your administration and give options as to where you would like to accept extra teaching duties, things can work out in your favour. Be willing to negotiate and go into this with an open mind. At times, you may be faced with tasks that don't quite suit you, but think about how you can learn from these experiences for the future. Be a giver, and the world (and your classroom) will be a better place for it.

Getting involved can be done effectively on a micro level on a day-to-day basis with your students. One way I have found to be highly effective is to sit down during the lunch break and actually eat your lunch with them. At most schools I have worked at, there has been a designated period of time (ten or fifteen minutes) in which the students are required to sit down and eat their lunch. Usually by this time, I am so hungry myself that I would begin to eat with the students. This became a ritual where we would sit and eat and talk about things other than what was going on in the classroom.

My students would ask for advice about life and things that were important to them, no matter what age they were. This enabled me to learn a little bit about them as people and to build a sense of comradery and trust that really made my job worthwhile. If I was teaching younger children, like preschoolers, they would most often sit cross-legged on a floor space somewhere. I would instinctively sit cross-legged with them to give a sense that even though I was still the teacher, we were all on the same level.

This reminds me of a funny story that happened a few years ago when I was a preschool teacher. One day, one of the students refused to eat his lunch. Apparently, as it is with children of this age, the bread didn't look right or his mother hadn't blessed it properly or some such thing. As a teacher of this age group, you hear the strangest (and funniest) reasons why something is or isn't right. I can almost feel all the preschool teachers in the world nodding their heads in approval at this statement whist trying not to laugh at the silliness of it all.

Anyway, this particular student wouldn't eat his lunch, and after a very tense couple of minutes of trying to persuade him, I became quite cranky (as most adults do at some point). I was racking my brain trying to figure out what the magic formula was for making him eat his lunch. As all legendary teachers know, there is in 99 per cent of cases a magic word or phrase or threat that can move mountains. So in desperation, I blurted out that if he wanted to be big and strong like me, then he had just better well eat his lunch. With tear-filled eyes, this child eventually succumbed to the pressure and began to eat.

I sat down rather mystified and exhausted to eat my own lunch. Another child approached and reassured me that I had said the right thing: "It's a good thing that you told him he was going to grow up to be big and strong like you, because you are big and strong, Mr. P."

This situation makes me laugh even to this day as I write this. It typifies all the genuineness that students will bring to you and your classroom when you bring it yourself. Your students are no fools—especially young children. They will see straight through you and everything you stand for in an instant. So be mindful of your words, deeds, and intentions at all times, because believe it or not, they are always watching, listening, and absorbing everything about you as their teacher, their role model, and their leader.

Another way to get involved is to sit and just talk with your students during your own time. I have spent many lunch breaks sitting and talking to my students in an informal manner. I have obviously followed professional lines with the conversations, but it's interesting the things I've learned about my students through this and how it has helped me to understand their world better. The more you make yourself available to chat informally with your students in an appropriate setting, the more they will develop a genuine respect for the fact that you really do care for their education and their welfare.

Now, many teachers will scoff at this and say it is just not possible with time constraints and professional responsibilities, but just like anything, if you believe in it, you can find the time. I'm not advocating that you spend every lunch break doing this; start with one a week or even one every couple of weeks and go from there. Perhaps even start you own conversation and social speaking club. Create a space in your classroom or school where students can meet and make new friends and discuss and share different topics. Unlike subjects like debating, there is no winner or loser. Everyone can contribute as much or as little as they choose. Some students may just want to listen in, whilst others just want someone to listen.

This can even run in conjunction with a peer support or school buddy program. As we all know, there are a lot of students out there who just want to be part of something and to be made to feel special. I know that I have stated this many times in this book also, but only because I truly believe in it. Experiment with this and even meditate on some new variations. Be creative and open to any possibilities, because they do exist.

Another big part of getting involved is to become a leader in a particular field of education. This is as easy as finding an aspect of teaching that you have a particular interest in or a passion for and expanding on this. You can be unbelievably brave and dive head first into something that you know nothing about, or you can expand on an area of expertise.

In my teaching journey, I have done a bit of both. The one thing I did find interesting that, according to the experts, is that for most people public speaking is rated scarier than death. Teaching will give you a truckload of opportunities to become good at this (the public speaking bit not the dying bit). Of all the skills it takes to be a legendary teacher, this is the one skill that can really open doors for you. Once you get past the fear factor (which stems from making mistakes in front of people), you are set.

I can recall the very first time I had to stand up at a staff meeting and present some highly uninteresting educational facts to the rest of the day care centre staff. I was so nervous that my left eye began to twitch. At one point, I thought it was going to pop right out of its socket. My supervisor knew I was really nervous but encouraged me to keep making more presentations at more meetings in front of different types of audiences. After a year or two, I had become a seasoned campaigner, and this allowed me to really sharpen my public relations skills in other areas also. To the point where I seemed to be able to create a unique sense of confidence not only within myself but also within my preschool students, their parents, and all the other centre staff.

Another valuable lesson I learned from this was that schools and other educational organisations absolutely love teachers who have a fantastic sense of self-confidence and great public relations skills. This in the long term has brought me fantastic promotions and job offers that allowed me to continually break through new personal barriers and work in a myriad of different educational settings. The key here is to be the shining light that can push through fear and let others know that you can be relied upon to get the job done (even if you scare the daylights out of yourself as you do it).

The best thing about being involved in any kind of volunteer work, either at your school or within your community, is that when it is enjoyable and straight from the heart, it never really feels like work. When your students and fellow staff members see you out there having a go and putting your heart into it, it's amazing how much extra help the universe can seem to drum up for you. When you get to the end of your teaching life, you will be amazed at how many things you have contributed to along the way. As I have discovered, even for the teaching journey itself, nothing looks more impressive on your teaching CV than all the volunteer work you have done.

CHAPTER 9

BE YOURSELF

B EING YOURSELF AS a teacher involves the key aspect of being a lifelong learner. Being committed to lifelong learning is something that, like any skill, involves practice and dedication.

An important part of your teaching journey is establishing your teaching character. When I first began teaching, I honestly didn't think this aspect of my teaching was very important, but as the years rolled by, I realised it allowed me to define who I was and what I truly believe as a teacher. Yet it generally came from the perceptions of others about who I was.

To explain this a little further, I was always encouraged by my mother's notion that there can be never enough silliness and fun in the world—or in one's teaching. Not that I wanted my classroom to represent a circus tent or a comedy club, but there had to be certain aspects of fun that ultimately made me feel comfortable with my teaching but at the same time allowed my students to find themselves. Yet at first, I believed that a teacher should be like a drill sergeant. I tried to emulate R. Lee Emery's character of Drill Sergeant Hartman from Stanley Kubrick's film *Full Metal Jacket*. This was the no-nonsense, authoritarian teaching style that I really believed the teaching world needed. I actually practiced his movements and body language for a couple of years early on.

This type of teaching style did in fact have its place in my teaching world. It did set a "don't mess with me" precedent with my students, which did help them achieve great results for their own self-discipline. To this day, I still use Sgt. Hartman's line "I am tough but I am fair" with all my new students. Perhaps this goes back to my own childhood, where I saw figures of authority as not to be trifled with.

But there are other aspects of my teaching style that stem from very different characters. Another I loved to emulate was Benjamin Franklin "Hawkeye" Pearce's character from the TV series *M*A*S*H*, played by Alan Alda. This character was highly intelligent and highly regarded but seemed to be stuck in a no-win situation between what he believed and what he was forced to endure. To remedy this (or at least cope with it), Hawkeye used humour to override the sense of bureaucratic incompetence that pervaded every aspect of his day-to-day life. This being that he had to cope with both being in the army against his will and being in a warzone. In my teaching, I have experienced things that have shook me right down to my core. At times, I have been severely conflicted about where my teaching life was going and how the powers of authority can present totally unworkable situations. I have used humour to give myself the emotional out that I needed to make the impossible seem possible.

Both of the characters mentioned above are from the military, and I have always seen the teaching game as being much the same. There is a chain of command and hierarchy just like any other organisation. At times, teaching, just like the military, requires blind obedience to get the job done. Just like the military, there is a sense of structure to hold everything together. At times, this structure has served me well, and at other times not so well. But without the structure, there would be total chaos. And in a state of total chaos, nobody wins—not your students and especially not you the teacher.

To lighten the mood just a tad, I would like to describe the third character that makes up my teaching persona. That is the character of Basil Fawlty from the hit BBC-TV series *Fawlty Towers*, played be

John Cleese. Basil is a character I seem to relate to and emulate when things are so crazy in my classroom they become laughable. That has been the real trick for me as a teacher: to stop, take a step back, laugh at myself, and make fun of the unworkable or impossible situations that once again we all seem to encounter in our teaching life.

I encourage you to seek out your teaching character. Find the person you are meant to be and be that person. Add humour, wit, craziness, and whatever else it takes to win the respect of your students and colleagues, and go with it. Be daring and experiment with different character approaches. Make it into a theatrical production if you wish.

I once heard a legendary teacher describe teaching as being exactly the same as acting. So act the part and be who it is you would like to be. Dress up and be noticed, if you will. Be courageous and adventurous in any way you choose. Remember that as long as it's legal, moral, and ethical, and you adhere to your teaching code of conduct, you can pretty much do as you please to make it work for you. I can't encourage you enough to do this with all you heart.

I would like to emphasise this point by sharing a personal story about the very first time I ever went ice skating. I was twenty-two years old and had just completed the first year of my early childhood bachelor's degree. I came away from that first year of university with many new learning experiences and was keen to put this into practice in others aspects of my life.

My sister Mandy invited me one evening to go ice skating with the local church youth group. At first I thought, *No way,* but then something deep inside me told me this could be fun. Though I spent more time that evening sliding across the ice face-first than I did actually skating on it, I remember that something captivated me enough that I wanted to master this skill and be good at it—or at least competent.

There was a huge banner in the rink saying that beginner skating classes were about to begin. I knew that was my cue. A week or so later, I stood quivering with fear (and embarrassment) on the ice with a large group of children ranging in age from five to ten. I said to the instructor, who happened to be an Australian figure skating champion, that I'd made a big mistake joining the learn-to-skate class and that I needed to leave. She looked me straight in the eye and said that she wanted me to skate towards her, and she would catch me. After watching all the children do it, I thought I could do it too.

Now to paint an even more imposing scene, this particular ice rink was located right smack bang in the middle of a huge shopping centre (mall) and was also overlooked by a McDonald's and a movie theatre. As I timidly skated (shuffled) towards my skating teacher, I could feel a thousand eyes watching me thinking, *What the hell is that guy doing there?* As I got to my teacher, I promptly collapsed into her arms. She was stronger than she looked, and she actually caught me and held me upright. I apologised profusely and began to berate myself for being so clumsy. She again looked me straight in the eyes like God herself and, with total confidence, said to me that I would get there.

I told her how embarrassed I felt trying to learn to skate in front of all these kids and shoppers, and she said something that I will never forget. She said that out of all the people watching me in that moment, most of them would be too scared to do what I was doing right now. The fact that I was there after signing up to learn to skate meant that I was serious about pushing myself as a person. She then gently pushed me back towards the boards, and all the children clapped me on encouragingly. I nearly cried.

Four years later, after many more falls and lots more practice, I was playing ice hockey at the highest senior level, which also included a stint at university in Canada. I went back to that ice rink a few years after that and was casually skating around when my beginning skating teacher glided up next to me. She told me how she was watching me skate and couldn't believe that it was really me. I told her that her kind words during that first lesson were what spurred me on to keep practicing and enjoying learning this new skill (which included playing ice hockey and a little later speed skating).

That's how I learned about the power of self-belief. Believe in yourself as a teacher, and more importantly, believe in yourself as a learner. Remember that everyone who is learning absolutely anything must always start at the beginning.

When I began my teaching life in preschool, I soon realised that many small children try to hide their fear of not looking competent. This included fear of simple things like talking to others or of asking for help or even going to the toilet. This was when I remembered how that ice skating teacher acted when she was teaching me to skate. She showed kindness and compassion and understanding to help me, her student, to succeed.

As much as we need to show these fantastic traits to our students, we need to also show them to ourselves. As a teacher, you benefit greatly by being your own teacher and guide. Reflect on your own approach to yourself and give yourself all the pep talks and confidence boosters you need (and believe me, you will need them). Be your own best friend and support, and most importantly, after you make some huge mistake, forgive yourself and be open to many more learning experiences.

One of the most important aspects of being yourself in the teaching industry is to take your teaching job seriously. You are entrusted with the very responsible task of educating the next generation of children or even the next wave of young adults. For this, you need to know that everything you do as a teacher is important as far as taking yourself seriously. You need to respect the role that you have been given and develop a deep sense of gratitude for the job you have or are about to be undertaking.

The strangest thing in our society is how people react when I tell them I am a teacher. At first, most people are surprised, and then after I tell them that I spent almost 15 years as a preschool teacher, this turns into a kind of bemusement. One thing a lot of people say is that it is a tough job that they feel they could never do. And the sad thing is that generally people don't show a huge amount of respect for this position, even though it is a tough job. I find that general respect for early childhood educators is lacking in our society somewhat. Yes, this is only my perception but it seems to me that the higher the age level that you teach the more respect you seem to get.

You will have to develop a lot of skills over many years to really understand and appreciate what type of teaching actually suits you. Just like Regina Brett states in her fantastic book *God Is Always Hiring*, it's about finding meaning in your teaching job and believing that God, the universe, your guardian angels, or whatever it is that you choose to believe in is leading you there. Teaching takes a lot of faith, which will come from the strangest places within you.

I have complete faith that as a teacher, you always be in the right place to learn the right thing. All things connected to my teaching, especially the not-so-good situations, have served their purpose right alongside all the things that were deemed good experiences. As much as we don't want to go through our teaching lives having one bad experience after another, we need to take these on the chin and always believe that our higher power has our best interests at heart.

There will be times when your teaching role will push you to the edge of sanity. I have always believed that this is God enabling me to fully experience where my personal and professional limits are so I know they are there. Unfortunately, many new teachers or teachers in general find this process unbelievably scary, to the point where they would almost run in the opposite direction from fear. But if you want to find your teaching treasure, you'd better be prepared to do some serious spiritual digging into who you are and what you hold sacred within you own abilities.

This doesn't mean you will just snap your fingers and have it all figured out. It takes courage on a grand scale to explore, expand, and go where you've never been before. This can be a physical entity but mostly involves you being brave enough to keep trying new things within your teaching to find your perfect fit. I used to describe this feeling to my mother, who is also a teacher, as being in my groove. I use this metaphor to describe when everything you're doing in your teaching feels right because it is right. The groove bit comes from that sound when a record needle (I'm showing my age here) finds a groove on the record and the music flows beautifully.

Your ability to own your own teaching is critical to your long-term survival as a teacher. I have been through some fantastic teaching situations that allowed me to embrace this and blossom, and I have been through others that quite clearly did *not*. It's like anything in life: you have good years and challenging years, great classes and classes you'd prefer to see at the bottom of the ocean. For teachers, it's not about getting to work in a good school or trying to get that good class with good students. That is all very nice, but it's not how the teaching universe works. I believe the teaching gods always put you in a situation that allows you to both learn and experience something. And I truly believe that if you open yourself up to this wisdom, you will find yourself in the right situation for you. And again I have stated this many times in this book too and once again, only because I truly believe it (for myself and of course for you also).

What's right for you is not necessarily right for someone else. Teachers are always looking and striving for their niche, and this could be literally anywhere within the industry or anywhere on this planet. Be the seeker of experiences and challenges, not the one who yearns to gain recognition and status. As the Bible states, "God opposes the proud and gives grace to the humble" (James 4:6 NIV). I've been around long enough to know this quote inside out and have seen this way too many times in my teaching life not to believe it.

Be a leader in your field who isn't scared of a challenge ... or yes, you can be scared, but do it anyway. Do not allow fear to dictate your life as a teacher. Fear can be your friend rather than your enemy. As a friend, fear allows you to instinctively know how to avoid situations that are not in your best interests. This could be through knowing your code of conduct and being able to tell potentially disastrous situations from beneficial ones.

The images of teachers in the media are seldom good or positive. Stories of teachers being assaulted and students doing drugs or whatever are the norm. Positive stories rarely get a look. But the good news is that you can live your own good-will story by not believing this sensational rubbish and inventing and living out your own version of who you really want to be as a teacher and a role model.

Self-belief as a teacher is the first step to enabling yourself to achieve greatness with your students. It's not about scoring political points with anyone or getting to the top of some popularity contest, but rather being genuine about who you are as a teacher, what you're doing, and where it is you are taking your students.

This may all sound again like some sort of motivational pep talk, and I guess in a lot of ways that's exactly what you will need to survive day to day in this job. And like every fantastic skill you will need to say it, hear it and practice many times over to get it just right. I wake up every day and go to bat for myself. I tell myself I am part of something really fantastic and something truly wonderful in the teaching world (and the world itself). I know that my sincere efforts as a teacher are shaping the next generation of competent, well-adjusted, and well-balanced people who are committed to themselves and their own goals and aspirations. They have been taught to be responsible for their own words, actions, and thoughts. That makes me feel worthwhile and important in my journey as a legendary teacher. And so it can be for you too. You just have to believe in yourself and your abilities.

To all you millennials out there who are currently teaching, studying teaching, or even just thinking about teaching: you are not going to start your career at the top. You will be cutting your teeth on many different challenges that at times will feel like they are never-ending, but with patience, perseverance, and a good dose of persistence, you will find these experiences will give you the necessary grit to get you to the next level. And it does take grit, believe me.

You will have discussions with your friends who are working in IT or as engineers and are earning in a day what you make in a week. Be happy for these people, as their skills are just as important as yours. But be content in the knowledge that what you sow as a teacher can never be outdated or downsized or boring. You take your clients on a magical journey every day to places they could only ever dream of. If you are lucky enough like me to love teaching young children, the blessings just keep coming. They can be measured in generations and even lifetimes.

Most teachers unfortunately don't seem to grasp this concept of wanting to make a difference in others people's lives. This is the foundation of everything that our human race depends upon for its survival. Education is the one aspect that can make or break a family, a village, a town, an organisation, or even a society. The more you tune in to how important your role is as a teacher, the more respect you will earn from your students of any age.

Please keep in mind that being yourself in a profession like teaching is fraught with danger. The biggest that I have ever faced is ridicule by other teachers. Teachers deal with facts and figures and curricula and outcomes. Anything that falls beyond that scope is dismissed as unimportant. New ideas (or old ones re-engineered) are not particularly welcomed. I would go so far as to say that I have seen teachers continually working with unproductive ideas, unwilling to change because it's too hard. The big one I hear a lot these days is "I will stick this out until I retire" or something similar.

A big part of being yourself as a teacher is to be continually growing, developing and moving forwards. If you are stagnating in your teaching life, then you are dying. It's that simple. Be proactive in always being on the lookout for new pathways in which to teach. Remember, there are no silly ideas but rather teachers who are too scared or too insecure within themselves to try them. Be a pioneer of new thought in education on whatever level you are at.

I have heard from many teachers over the years that the only way to change a system is to crawl your way to the top and begin there.

I say that the only way to change a system is to begin at the bottom, where all the young and impressionable minds are. As Mahatma Gandhi so famously said it once again, "Be the change you want to see in the world."

To tell you the honest truth, I didn't actually believe that when I first heard it. I thought it was some fluffy statement reserved for those with status and privilege. But over the years, it grew on me, until I realised one day that the positive changes I had consciously made in my own life began to flow into my teaching. I became it, and it became me. It was like a metamorphosis that seemed to permeate every aspect of what I believed as a person and as a teacher.

You will come up against teaching critics of all shapes and sizes. When facing these people, just be respectful, defend your position, send lots of love and forgiveness, and move on. Remember that in this lifetime, you don't have to agree with everyone. Differences in opinion are not worth starting a war over.

Teaching, like any profession, involves learning many different skills. These skills cannot, unfortunately, all be learned at once or in the first year of teaching. You will come across many know-it-all teachers, and you will come across others who may not have a clue about anything. Follow your gut instinct to what works for you and your teaching. Experiment with different approaches and procedures. You do have to follow the set curriculum for where you are and adhere to a professional code of conduct, but work the rest of it to your advantage. You will find that in some schools, you won't fit in with the vision, and at others, you will thrive. That's all okay; you are there to gain valuable knowledge about who you are and perhaps which direction you want to go.

This leads me to the notion of goal-setting. There is a popular train of thought that if you don't have any teaching goals, you are floundering and going nowhere. Administrations are obsessed with goal-setting. Some of it useful, but in my experience, most of it is not. Most of the best teaching goals that I have ever achieved just happened by themselves. I had plenty of vision and focused on what was important to me both as a teacher and as a person, and this created options from which my goals stemmed.

I have written down many goals over the years, and 80 to 90 per cent of those never happened. This for a long time left me feeling discouraged and deflated, until it finally dawned on me that the 10 to 20 per cent that did eventuate were far better than the original goals I had in mind for myself.

You may agree or disagree with some or all of this, but I am just sharing a different perspective from my many teaching and life experiences. As Tony Robbins puts it so eloquently in his fantastic book *Unlimited Power*, "Sow a dream and reap a destiny." As a teacher, you are doing just that: reaping your destiny. Get aligned with yourself, and you will know where and when you are meant to do your teaching. Couple this with openness that you will always be at the right place and the right time. Even if this leads you to a not-so-positive teaching situation, be positive and look for the key skills you will learn from this.

Too many teachers walk around talking about their ideal teaching situation or school or class or whatever. Unfortunately, I must tell you that this doesn't exist. There are situations that are more advantageous to you at times, but like everything else, they are just learning experiences. The bad experiences never last, but then again, neither do the good ones. Each teaching year or situation will bring its own lessons to you, and I would encourage you to be open to the universe's way of teaching you this.

Everything has it season or phase or whatever, and then it moves on. Don't get caught in the trap of thinking that a better teaching job is just around the corner or that you can't wait to go and work in a good school or you can't wait to retire. The teaching and the learning begin right where you are. There is no pot of gold at the end of the rainbow, because you are already there. To your school and your students, you are the pot of gold. You are the source of their inspiration. Begin by inspiring yourself. Push yourself to believe in yourself. Push yourself into wanting a better world for your students (and yourself).

Creating these options is as simple as making a decision about something you've always wanted to do. If you're just starting out or are in a transitory phase of your teaching, simply put it out there to God or the universe or whatever higher power you believe in and let it guide you to your goals. This may sound very spiritual, but the fact is that teaching, like many other professions, is undergoing a big spiritual overhaul. Teachers are tuning in to a bigger picture that involves forces beyond their control.

Seek out legendary teachers to help you along in your journey of discovery. They will be more than happy to mentor you and guide you through the many challenges you will face. And you, in turn, will pass this invaluable knowledge on to someone else down the track.

One of the hardest aspects to being yourself is understanding how you fit into the mould of being a teacher. Each school, college, or learning institution has a certain set of procedures or unwritten rules or guidelines a teacher has to abide by. Learning these can be a system of trial and error, as you find your own way of doing things. Some of these procedures come in a very specific written form and can even be part of a contract you will actually have to sign and agree to abide by to remain in your teaching job. Others are not so specific but are equally important for your survival in that particular teaching culture. But whatever the expectations or procedures, you will still need to own your own teaching and, more importantly, be open to continually learning about yourself.

This comes in the form of adopting a continual growth mindset. This is a mindset where you are continually learning and moulding both who you are as a teacher and how you do the actual teaching. I will go through these step by step with what I have experienced and how these may benefit you in your teaching journey also.

One of the most important rules of teaching is not to become complacent. I admit that I have been guilty of breaking this rule many times. Teaching is like life itself: always changing, growing, and evolving. As we experience great things with our students, there is an illusion that these fantastic experiences will last forever. Unfortunately, this is not so. Great things can, will, and do happen, but they are fleeting moments in the great labyrinth that is your teaching life.

Some experiences will inspire you, and others will make you question your sanity. Like the yin and yang of teaching, they live side by side to give you a taste of everything at your teaching banquet. Obviously, as time goes on and you gain more of an idea of yourself, you will strive for more positive experiences than negative to keep you going. Ironically, some of my most negative experiences in teaching have become, in themselves, my best teachers. They allowed me to see my flaws and negative teaching traits for exactly what they were: areas in need of correction. The beauty of teaching is that these opportunities for correction can come at any time and in any place along the way.

This is where an open mind comes into play. Having an open mind with your teaching and indeed yourself as a person will be the single most important factor in determining your contentment and fulfilment as a teacher. This can become like an inner radar that determines whether your teaching approach is taking a positive direction or a negative one. Tune in to this inner radar, and it will give you that heartfelt feeling of know what is or isn't right for you as you travel along on your teaching journey.

The important part of being yourself is knowing yourself. One of the best books I have ever had the privilege of reading was Gary Chapman's *The Five Love Languages*. As much as this book was originally intended for helping people in personal relationships, I found it very helpful in my professional teaching life also. I found that my number-one love language was touch, and this is how I truly expressed myself to those around me that I felt deeply for.

Then I became a male preschool teacher, and the word *touch* had a very negative connotation in that professional realm. As a male, I was constantly drilled about the million or so different ways I could be seen as some kind of pervert or weirdo when working with such young children. Now, twenty-two years into my teaching journey, there are still many teachers who think that men have no place near young children. Almost every year, I get chastised or dragged over the proverbial coals about my interactions with my students, especially when it comes to how teachers conduct themselves with students in the form of appropriate touch.

Before I really get into this topic, I must explain that I wasn't sure how to even approach it in this book. After consulting many of my mentors, I got everything from "Don't even go there" to "It's your book; write what you are passionate about." So I will endeavour to explain each point very carefully and succinctly to avoid any confusion or misinterpretation. I know deep down in my heart that there will be a very small percentage of teachers who will complain about this anyway. I suggest that they go out and find someone to give a hug to.

Back to the issue at hand. As a person with touch at the top of my love language list, I found myself in the very strange position of teaching preschool children and trying to keep an element of professionalism in how I interacted with them. Anyone who has ever taught preschool or day care will know that not a day goes by when there is not someone—either adult or child—who needs a pat on the back or even a hug. In a nurturing profession like early childhood education, these things become a given.

Additionally, as a male, I found myself becoming purely, by default, a human climbing frame. Any male, parent or teacher, who is in close proximity to young children will find themselves in a similar position. Every time I would bend down to either talk to a child or tie someone's shoelaces or whatever, there was always another child waiting to literally jump on my back. When it came to story time, there was a line-up of children who wanted desperately to sit on my lap. Now, as a male and as a professional, this kind of behaviour from my students made me very uncomfortable. To the point where I was so paranoid about being accused of something that I didn't even want to step foot through the door each day.

I consulted my preschool director and asked what her thoughts were on this subject. She explained to me, as have many directors since, that the children trusted me and were just showing their natural appreciation for me. After a couple of years of proving myself to the staff and parents, it became a very different place. I even recall that after I was appointed director of one day care centre, parents would bring their children through the main door each morning, march them to my office door, and instruct them to give me a hug to start the day. This showed their trust towards me at the highest level. I always appreciated this and never ever forgot these kind gestures. Unfortunately, the most bizarre incidents with parents and children were yet to come.

Being yourself within your teaching should come from a place of love within you and not fear. The one aspect of myself I had to overcome as a male preschool teacher was the fear of being accused of something. But as teaching preschool was something I felt called to do, I made a constant commitment to myself to overcome this fear.

I recall as a beginning teacher being told to record everything to cover myself against litigation. I would instruct all beginning teachers to do the same. But as you gain more experience as a teacher, you will inevitably gain a greater insight into what is worth documenting and what isn't. The strangest thing I have encountered as a teacher is that what seem to me to be the worst case scenarios for me seem to go nowhere. And what seem to others to be the worst scenarios were at times things I couldn't even remember. In some very rare cases, the students even made up a story and lied about a situation.

The key is to just roll with it and do your best. Keep in mind that the biggest complainers will be your students' parents. Some— usually a very small percentage—will complain that the grass is too green and the sky is too blue; you will never be able to please them. Just wave and smile and apologise and then get back to work. Mostly, these individuals want someone to vent to, and you unfortunately are perceived to be the only person in their world who is paid to listen to them. Be polite and always show courtesy—and when in doubt, call for help.

Never feel obliged to listen to endless ranting. Know your place and stand your ground if you feel threatened. You can always ask the individual to leave if you feel unsafe. A good policy is to consult other teachers and staff and have them on standby if you feel a situation with a parent could become uncomfortable. Please be aware of these aspects of teaching, and if you are experiencing any difficulties in any of these situations, consult your admin straight away.

The golden rule is to never be in a classroom where you are with a student alone, even if the student is injured or unconscious. Always find someone to be a witness to any interaction that requires first aid on any level. If you have to, ask other students to stand there and watch. I have had many instances where I have asked parents, students, and other teachers to stay with me and be my witnesses. I have even gone so far as to explain why I need them to be there. In 99 per cent of cases, they have been happy to stay and support me. In the 1 per cent, where I have been on my own, I left the student briefly to find someone else. First aid providers will always tell you never to leave patients on their own, but I feel safer with someone else with me (especially if I will need assistance moving a student to a safer place). Realistically, it's very unlikely that you will ever be in a situation as a teacher where you are totally alone without any assistance.

Another good practice is to become aware of potential situations before they arise. If you are on an excursion or a camp with your students, make yourself aware of any potential threats of the physical but also legal kind. Not that I want to make you totally paranoid about what may happen, but just be aware.

I recall back when I was in my final year of my early childhood degree, we had a visit from the police as part of a child-protection subject. The police were very informative and very direct, but they did make a point of aiming a lot of their directives at me, or so I thought. I put up my hand and questioned the detective on this, and she said that the media and our society in general will pick on me because I am a male.

After this, I felt like quitting teaching and switching to another degree. The only thing that saved me was my senior lecturer, who was a former preschool teacher herself. She told me that if I was really passionate about being an early childhood teacher—and she knew I was—I should just run with that. Once I got into teaching, I would be so busy that I wouldn't have time to worry about being sued by someone. Once again let your teaching come from a place within you of love and passion and not of fear and doubt.

Back on the subject of appropriate touch with students, I will share these personal experiences as a male early childhood teacher. In my first teaching job in a preschool, I was totally paranoid and very reserved around my students, especially as appropriate touch was concerned. I felt like everyone was watching me and waiting for me to slip up or do something inappropriate, especially since I was the lone male teacher. I was constantly asked why I, as a man, wanted to work with young children.

After a few years, I realised that my main task as a preschool teacher was to be comfortable in my own skin and roll with whatever situations came to hand. I needed to be highly professional, but I also needed to add a human touch to my teaching, especially with young children. This was when the preschoolers began to insist on holding my hand during outdoor supervision times. They would also sit right next to me when listening to a story being read. Eventually, I got to that point where I became the human climbing frame as I described before. Earning their trust paved the way for lots of positive, appropriate touch. If anything was ever deemed inappropriate, it was documented and witnessed by as many other staff members as I could find.

Being that this was a preschool, we had young children learning to toilet train. The rule in preschools and day cares is that if you find it, you deal with it. I found plenty of situations where I cleaned up indescribable messes that came out of both ends of a child. When I had proven myself with my fellow staff members by doing this, the women I worked with were more than happy vouch for my genuine love of being a teacher and wanting to be a positive role model.

I still go to school every day and have students of all ages run (sometimes from across the school) to hug me. I still get complaints from other teachers and occasionally parents about this, to which I have two replies. Firstly, it's the students who want to hug me (not that I mind, because I love hugs); and secondly, if children don't feel secure around a teacher, or anyone adult for that matter, they generally don't run towards them and give them a hug. Perhaps the appropriate point here is that a legendary teacher always knows the value of appropriate touch when teaching students.

The authors of the teaching textbook *Human Relations Development: A Manual for Educators* suggest that appropriate physical touch with students can have huge positive outcomes for the children's sense of belonging and well-being. In her wonderful book *The Little Book of Hugs*, Kathleen Keating points how non-sexual, well-intended hugs can have huge benefits for everybody involved. She states that you must always ask for permission before approaching someone for a hug, which I feel is highly sensible and appropriate in the correct teaching situation. I actually explain this to my students and then describe the complex variety of hugs and how they can be used in each appropriate setting.

As for me, any of my students past or present or even future always have my permission to give me a hug anytime. The funny thing is, they always do. I have always had students wanting to hug me throughout my teaching life. I have former preschool students who are now adults hugging me in supermarkets, gyms, churches, and other public places.

This reminds me of the story of the hugging judge I read about years ago in Jack Canfield's *Chicken Soup for the Soul*. Lee Shapiro was a retired judge in the United States who used to walk around offering people free appropriate hugs. When asked why, he said that a hug is an innocent form of appropriate human touch, and it's what the world needs more of. To my knowledge, I don't recall this having a negative effect on the people he hugged, nor did anyone try to sue him over being inappropriate.

I also saw a story on the news a few years back about a young indigenous girl named Jasirah who came from remote North Western Australia. She decided to stand on a crowded beach with a blindfold on and a sign saying, "I trust you. Do you trust me? Let's hug." She later told reporters that her aim was to bridge the gap between indigenous and non-indigenous people by way of the most affective human behaviour: a hug. If you would like to see this for yourself plus many other extraordinary examples of this type of social experiment from around the world, go to youtube.com and type in *blind trust experiment*. I have viewed this just now, and I couldn't stop crying as I watched this brave act.

As a teacher, I participate in this brave act everyday of my working life by allowing my students the honour of hugging me. Many of my teaching colleagues have warned me that such behaviour is highly inappropriate and even unprofessional. I just say that if my students wish to hug me in an appropriate manner, I will never turn them away.

I recall many years ago being at a school where the principal ushered me into his office. He was noticeably embarrassed about what he had to do. I respected him greatly, and my intuition told me what was coming. Although he was also an affectionate person and a dad himself, he told me in no uncertain terms not to hug the students anymore. I calmly explained that I didn't really hug anybody; I just allowed the students to hug me. Since we had at that time about 50 per cent indigenous students, they were mainly the ones who wanted to hug me, as they didn't get a lot of positive and appropriate touch from adults in their lives. The principal restated his position on this, even though I knew he didn't really believe it himself.

I then asked sincerely what I was to do when a child approached me with an intent to give me a hug. Students generally ran towards me smiling with their arms outstretched. The principal was at first a bit baffled by this question; I think he just thought I would say "yes, sir" and go about the rest of my teaching day. He finally said in a very stern voice that I was to instruct them that they were not to do so. I left his office soon after with this strange notion of how the heck I was going to get over a hundred preschoolers not to ever come near me or hug me ever again.

As I walked towards my classroom, a small indigenous female student came running up to me and tried to hug me. I put out my hand out as if to say no—as the words were about to leave my mouth—when my hand caught her under the chin. To stop her from falling backwards and cracking her head on the concrete path, I instinctively grabbed the front of her school shirt to hold her up. She took this to be part of a game, laughed along with it, and hugged me anyway. She even told all her friends about what had happened.

I decided that this was going to be my last year at this particular school anyway, and I rode out the last six months trying to dodge a horde of children trying to hug me. It was all very strange. On the last day I was there, I spent the last half hour of school with a huge line of about fifty to a hundred children of all ages demanding a final hug before I left that school. Many of these children were indigenous and said to me point-blank that they were going to give me hug and the admin couldn't do a thing to stop them.

The tears rolled down my cheeks during this experience. It was a really great feeling to be so appreciated by my students (and their brothers, sisters, cousins, and the like). It was like God and the universe were telling me that I was a legendary teacher.

Fast forward a couple of years. I'm at my next school. Again, I somehow managed to develop and invisible sign on top of my head saying to all the students, "Hugs, please." Again, my colleagues pointed out to me how inappropriate and unprofessional this was. I informed them that as a senior teacher, which I now was,

I was very much aware of what could be deemed inappropriate or unprofessional behaviour, and left it at that. I even spoke with several of my teacher aides and some of the parents whose children were amongst the main group of teacher huggers and asked them what they thought of this. They said that their children plus a huge horde of others absolutely loved me being their teacher and their positive role model, and that they were just expressing this with a form of appropriate physical touch.

Someone on my staff didn't see it that way, and again I was hauled in before the principal. I respected this principal greatly and knew, once again, what was about to be said. Again, he was a dad himself, and I knew he didn't really believe in what he was telling me, but was just, like the previous principal, covering himself and being seen to address the issue. Again I informed him that I didn't hug anyone but rather just allowed the students the freedom to hug me. He pointed out that it was inappropriate for even the high school kids to be hugging me, especially because most of them were girls.

I replied that I had taught all of these students in preschool many years earlier, and some of them I had known since they were babies and toddlers. The principal just told me not to do it anymore. I pointed out that all of these hugs occurred out in the open, mainly on the playground, and were not in some closed room somewhere. Again he said that I had been told and that I was to follow protocol.

There I was, a senior primary teacher who had come through the day care ranks as an early childhood preschool teacher and had shared hundreds of the best and worst of experiences with my students, their siblings, cousins, grandparents, aunties, uncles, and every one of their friends, now being told that my human touch that I was so proud of in my teaching was not allowed anymore. I remember walking out of that office feeling so dejected I was almost suicidal. I walked down to my classroom, and as I walked in the door, I nearly bumped into two female students leaving the adjacent classroom. They both looked at me with the most sympathetic faces and said that I looked like I needed a hug. I broke down and cried.

I don't recall much about the rest of that teaching day, as it was pretty forgettable. I came home and didn't really feel like being a teacher anymore. That evening, I downloaded an application to the Australian Federal Police, as I thought this would bring me the satisfaction I needed from a job by putting drug dealers and paedophiles behind bars. The next day, I even informed my admin of my intentions and said that it disappointed me greatly that the school didn't support their male teachers.

Unfortunately, physical touch has become a very contentious issue in education in recent years. It's actually almost bordering on a taboo subject on a lot of ways. Yes, students in the past have been physically, emotionally, and even sexually assaulted by teachers. The media loves to splash all this across the TV and internet every chance they get. The court cases against certain past teaching nuns and priests tell very sad story of how the Catholic Church has a lot of controversy now on its hands. Yet I have equally heard stories of wonderful teaching nuns and priests who in their service to God, gave the best of themselves to their students' education.

Anyway, as for me on my journey with this issue, God and the universe had a different plan. A couple of weeks later, we had our family festival at the school and I allocated myself to work at the fish and chips stall for this event. I recall seeing a huge group of past students forming in a line right in front of me. Some were teenagers and others were young adults. They were all students who, once again, I had taught in preschool many years before, plus some of their friends and siblings. I looked at them rather puzzled, wondering how so many of them could all be there at the festival at the same time and all be right in front of me at this stall in a line.

I asked to the first student, named Taylor, whether they wanted some fish and chips. She gave me this cheeky smile, like she knew what I needed. She said they weren't there for fish and chips; they all wanted to give me a hug. I spent the next ten to fifteen minutes chatting, hugging, laughing, and also towards the end crying with all of those little former preschoolers who were now in big people's bodies. All of this happened right in front of the admin staff. This was God and the universe's way of once again saying, "Adam Prociv, we officially proclaim you to be a legendary teacher and a legendary hugger." I'm even crying as I write this.

This also reminds me of another great story about hugs in schools. It was the first day of school in 2007. I was walking through the front gate of a State School here in Cairns. I had taken leave the previous year and done some travelling, and now after buying my first house I was ready to commence with preschool again, though it was now called prep.

So there I was, walking through the front gate, and no joke, I was confronted by a mob of about a hundred to a hundred and fifty people. About half were adults, and the rest were primary-school children of various ages. As I approached them, I recognised them as most of the students I had taught in preschool in previous years and of course their parents.

My first thoughts were, *Is this a protest of some kind? Are they having a meeting about something maybe?*

As I got closer, this huge cheer went up, and the crowd surged towards me. This startled me at first, but then something even more bizarre happened. As the children rushed forward to hug me, the parents actually pushed the children out of the way and also began hugging me. The principal saw all of this happen from her office window and later confessed to me that it was the most surreal event in education that she had ever witnessed, and she never would have believed it if she didn't see it with her own eyes.

An even stranger thing was yet to come. For that whole first week of school, every day my classroom door would be thrown open at various times of the day and a parent would barge into the classroom and proceed to hug me, often without any words being exchanged.

This was the point in my teaching journey where I really began to appreciate the amazing impact I'd had on this community, not only through my teaching but also through the power of appropriate touch and through hugs. This fantastic culture remains between myself and these students and parents today. To top it all off, this actually happened again a couple of hours before I began to write this section. I went to the main shopping centre in downtown Cairns and went into my favourite health food store. Low and behold, the young woman behind the counter was a former preschool student of mine named Julia. The first thing she did when she recognised me was to rush out from behind the counter and give me a big hug.

The best part about this was that she, like many others, became that little preschooler again. We talked about the great times we'd both had when I was her preschool teacher. This still brings tears to my eyes, even as I write this. Long live the days of play-based preschool and of teachers being able to give their students appropriate hugs.

I would also like to add yet another funny story about my "hugging" encounters. It's more like a series of stories over about three years, but I will condense it down into one. At the beginning of 2014, I was sent after nearly fifteen years of teaching preschool and prep to teach grade 4. Now, as an early childhood preschool teacher, I didn't know much about teaching the upper grades. I had done a couple of years as a contract teacher here and there, but nothing permanent. So I was thrown in with these big kids and forced to learn fast, which fortunately I am extremely good at. I had to make it up as I went along, which again, I am extremely good at. I remember distinctly saying to myself on the very first day of school that now I was in the big leagues of teaching, and that as these students were older (age nine or ten), I wouldn't be interacting with them the same way I did with the four-and five-year-olds. This obviously would include the absence of hugs. *No*, I thought to myself, *you won't be indulging in any of that soppy, wishy-washy nonsense with these guys. This is serious schooling, where they need to be taught appropriate boundaries.*

That little theory of mine lasted a couple of weeks at best, and then the floodgates opened once again and the hugs flowed freely between myself and my students. Even students from neighbouring grade 4 classrooms came and lined up to get their daily hug. I recall asking some of the parents several times if this seemed inappropriate in any way, and the response was always the same. They would tell me how their children came home each day and told fantastic stories about what they had learnt that day and how wonderful their teacher was.

These grade 4 students have all moved on, and the first batch are now in high school. What do you think is the first thing they do when they see me somewhere? You guessed it—they give me a big hug.

As you read this, you might be thinking that this guy is treading on very thin ice, especially in a professional sense. But the one thing I never do is shy away from who I am as a person or as a teacher. I do my very best to promote an atmosphere of love and acceptance for everybody I ever come into contact with, both personally and professionally. And good things always come to me in abundance.

And still on this point of appropriate touch with students I will now share a very different story that happened rather by accident. We were having an ANZAC Day parade a few years back at the school I was teaching at. I was sitting in the front row in the school auditorium with my class watching the proceedings. I noticed a teenage female Air Force cadet who was standing at attention on the stage. She began to sway very gently from side to side and about to faint. Suddenly I leapt out of my seat, lunged towards the stage, and put my hands out in front of me. This startled me somewhat, as I didn't really know why I did this until this young cadet passed out and fell off the stage (a metre or so high) directly into my arms.

If I had followed the no-touching rule that a lot of people seem to want to live by, I would have just let her fall to the hard wooden floor below. Even as I'm writing this, I cringe to think how badly injured that teenage girl would have been if I had done that. After I carried her unconscious in front of the whole school to the storeroom beside the stage, I was surprised (even shocked) that no other teachers followed me to assist. I still recall asking several teacher aides who were women to watch her and care for her, and I would supervise them.

Whilst we are on the subject of touch, an important part of this is to always keep your students safe. If they are in danger of any kind, do not hesitate to step in and either restrain or remove them from a dangerous or potentially dangerous situation. The online Queensland Law handbook states duty of care must be adhered to between a teacher and a student known to them. As a teacher and also as a professional, you are always legally bound to keep your students safe, whether this means escorting them away from a busy road, a brush fire or a beehive. They must follow your directives and instructions when needed.

On the rare occasion, you may even have to break up a fight. If you are very lucky, you may only have to do this once or twice in your teaching life. Use common sense; if you consider the situation too dangerous for yourself, then seek help. As a larger male, I have always been lucky with this. When the students involved in a fight have seen me coming, they generally know it's time to break it up. When in doubt, consult your school's code of conduct procedures. And once again never fear to call for back up.

CHAPTER 10

KEEP REINVENTING YOURSELF

I T TAKES A lot of personal energy to really discover who you are as a teacher and where you want to go. All legendary teachers know that the key to keeping yourself fresh and vibrant is to keep reinventing yourself. This is where the teaching profession can offer you the best opportunities for self-growth and self-discovery. It ultimately can be done in a number of different ways, which I will describe, but the key aspect to realise is especially if you are a beginning or even fairly new teacher, you can't learn everything and experience everything in the first year or so. It takes time and patience to develop and enhance your skills in the many areas you will need to be competent in. So prepare to learn the ropes and start at the bottom. Even as you do, you can rest easy that you won't be loaded with huge amounts of extra responsibility, and you can ease your way into how things are done and where you fit in the scheme of things.

Please also keep in mind, as a beginning teacher, that you are just that: at the beginning of something. Have the mindset that your first couple of years are like an apprenticeship, and you are well placed to learn from those around you who have walked the well-trodden path. If you are a mature-age beginning teacher and have some valuable life skills to offer, that's great, but please be aware that you are still at the beginning of your next life stage and need to be open to as many new ideas as possible. Trying to be a standout or a know-it-all will not do you or anyone around you any good. Do lots of listening and take lots of notes; this will enable you to keep an open mind about which direction you would like to go with your teaching.

A very important part of reinventing yourself as a teacher is to be prepared to be uncomfortable. Most teachers find the notion of being uncomfortable to be uncomfortable. We have developed this fear of the unknown. But being uncomfortable for brief periods in your teaching life will allow you to become more aware of what is going on around you. Be uncomfortable often enough, and you can develop a greater sense of your own awareness of new directions and new challenges. This all ties in beautifully with one of my favourite quotes by the Legendary U.C.L.A. Basketball Coach John Wooden. He said, "Things always turn out best for those that make the best of the way things turn out." I have found this so true for my own understanding of where I need to be teaching at any specific time and what I need to be learning about myself in the process.

Another key aspect of reinventing yourself is to shift your physical location from time to time. There is no hard and fast rule about when to move schools, colleges, towns, or cities, but a legendary teacher shifts to a new environment every couple of years to avoid going stale. As Tony Robbins states in his fantastic book *Awaken the Giant Within*, if something isn't constantly moving and growing, it's dying. Your teaching life can become like this very easily if you are not aware of your need for change.

You can make up as many excuses for not doing this as you want. You may have just gotten married or are about to have a baby or another baby or don't want to be too far away from your family. These are just excuses, and teachers like anybody else on this planet are very good at relying on them. The question to ask yourself is, "Do I want to have a safe life where not much changes, or do I want an exciting life where I am always ready for my next adventure?" Remember, as a teacher, you can work virtually anywhere on the planet. Take advantage of this great opportunity to move to new towns or cities or a new state or country. Take the leap and have faith that the universe will guide you every step of the way.

There may be some not-so-good experiences along the way, and there may be some outright disasters. But the most interesting legendary teachers I have ever met are the ones who can tell you about all of their crazy teaching experiences and still come up smiling. Most negative experiences are only good in hindsight, but that's the real essence of being a teacher: have courage and know that you can never fail at anything in your teaching life. There are just new phases of learning. Value your ability to become more resilient and to gather your courage and keep moving forwards.

I once heard a good quote that stated: "Think about what the average person would do and then do the opposite." That's exactly what I'm telling you to do here. How many teaching meetings do you go to where the back seats always seem to fill up first? And latecomers wouldn't dare try to cross a crowded room or sit in the front row. I would like to invite you to be that person who sits in the front row, even if it means sitting by yourself. I do it at every meeting I go to, even if I'm late. I simply walk in like I own the place and adopt the attitude that I am only human and lateness to a meeting is not a stoning offence.

The key is to think confidence, talk confidence, and really believe in your own confidence. Be the one to start a new trend of being a front-seater. Take some ideas along to spark some interesting conversation. Be open to what you can learn from a meeting and who you might meet there. Make it a game with yourself, and make it fun. You will get the odd negative teacher who tries to bring the energy of a meeting or gathering down. But as a positive teacher, be responsible for your own perceptions and believe that every opportunity, even a boring meeting, may bring you that much closer to a personal breakthrough or an idea that may send you in new directions.

Just today, I was in an after-school staff meeting watching a compulsory webinar on having a positive mindset. When I walked in, the whole mood of the meeting was sour, as most teachers don't really like having after-school meetings, even less so when such meetings involve watching something chosen by the administration. As I sat there observing the other teachers' body language, I made a decision that this webinar might give me some valuable insight into how I might change this. After I made this decision, my perceptions were totally different. I became immersed in the information that was being provided to me absolutely free of charge. All I had to do was sit and listen for an hour or so.

The captivating part of this presentation was how the concept of changing your mindset is a very simple one. As Dr. Wayne Dyer explains again in his book *Your Erroneous Zones*, making a decision to change your thought patterns in regards to adopting good habits is simple. Inevitably, the difficult part comes when you have to follow it up with hundreds or maybe even thousands of very simple little decisions over a period of time. This ultimately requires self-discipline and the willpower to know that you are always evolving and growing on your teaching journey and your life journey also.

Another important aspect of your teaching should be diversifying your area of expertise. I have over the years done many different types of teaching, mainly early childhood and primary. That's the beauty of teaching: you can move in many different directions once you gain a few years of experience. The best part is that you can just keep reinventing yourself and reincarnating yourself into whatever teacher you wish to be. There are no boundaries, and you can keep diversifying as much and as often as you wish.

Financial constraints may restrict you a little, especially if you are paying off a house, for example. But that should never be an excuse to not go somewhere. If you are in heavy debt, put a little bit of money aside for a short trip somewhere local. If you really believe this can be done, then it will be done. If you just sit there with your excuses, well, we all know how that ends.

I have been on many long and short trips to lots of different places. Some I just picked off the map for fun because I hadn't been there before. I have also gone on quite a few tours where I've met lots of interesting people (also teachers and travellers) who have opened my eyes to adventures that were once only part of my imagination. The best part about adopting a lifestyle such as this is the reward of going back to your school or college and sharing it all with your students. Nothing, and I mean nothing, beats inspiring young minds about the great wonders of our beautiful world as a person who has been there and continues to make plans to see more. It works. I love doing this with my own students on every trip I take.

Forget about fear of failure. Forget about what other people might think of you. The people you want to surround yourself with are likeminded souls who continually inspire you and are inspired by you. As Tony Robbins states in *Awaken the Giant Within*, he states that, "like attracts like and iron sharpens iron." Who knows who you will inspire along the way on your teaching journey? You may inspire your students and colleagues, and you may even inspire the parents of your students, especially if you are teaching young children.

Being yourself requires you as a teacher to form your own opinion of yourself, especially in your role as a teacher. Many new and beginning teachers struggle with the concept of how to form their own identity in the world of teaching. Many ideas and notions will be thrown at you—and in some cases imposed upon you—about what it is that you must know and ultimately teach. The modern teaching system, as we currently know it, is in my humble opinion trying its best to make every teacher teach to all students in exactly the same way.

This reminds me of the story of the rabbit who tried to climb a tree just to be like a possum and the fish who tried to walk on land just to be like the rabbit. They soon discovered that not only could they not do things as well as the other creatures, but in fact, they became less competent at their God-given gifts when they did. Teaching is just the same. If your strengths lay in a particular area of teaching, then go with that and excel.

You could always shake things up a bit and try something new, but know when you have hit your limitations. This will happen when your teaching stops being fun and starts to become a burden. The signs are there, and you must stay vigilant to know them when they arrive. It could be in the form of restless sleep or lack of motivation for your teaching job or lack of humour in your day-to-day teaching.

When things become too serious and you find yourself becoming irritable, it's time to re-assess your teaching position. This could mean finding a new grade to teach or transferring to a new school or whatever, but always be open to these options. Sometimes the universe deliberately places you in a bad situation to motivate you to learn something but also to get you to move on to something new. I have experienced this many times in my teaching life, and I have developed a keen sense of which situations work for me and which ones don't. Sometimes it takes people I trust to point this out to me also, but I know the signs when I see them in whatever form they are meant to take.

To be truly reinventing yourself, you will need two very important tools. The first is a childlike sense of wonder. Be in awe of this fabulous world that almighty God has created for us. Deliberately go out and find out about things you know absolutely nothing about, whether it be learning about bees or rocks or plants or whatever. And the second tool is always posing new questions to yourself about what it is that you wish to learn.

CHAPTER 11

HAVE FUN

D o you remember doing something in your life that was so boring it was agony to get through? And do you remember doing something that was an absolute joy and that seemed effortless? I won't say that teaching is definitely more like the latter, but it has to be a joy to do whilst challenging you and your limits. The aim of this book is to allow you to find and focus on the positive aspects of your teaching life and build on the experiences that really bring you joy.

Having fun is a sure-fire way to allow your creative energies to flow as a teacher whilst at the same time spreading positive energy throughout both your classroom and your workplace. Not that every day will be a laugh a minute and everybody will be walking on sunshine 24/7, but as the boss of your domain (your classroom), you can choose to bring a vibe of humour and fun to your teaching. Start by just getting to know your students on a fairly routine basis.

My grandmother told me something very important before I became a teacher. She said, "Adam, your students are just small individuals who don't know as much as you yet." I took this on-board and have always used it as a guideline for all the students I have taught, at any age level. They are still human beings just like me and have the same feelings, hopes and dreams as everybody else.

This has enabled me to meet my students where they are at regardless of age, background, or life experience. I tend to not make any quick judgements about who they really are until I get to know them a little. This is an important factor in creating success with my students, as it builds a solid foundation for good rapport. Without a good rapport, my teaching is going nowhere.

Getting to know your students will also allow you to get to know yourself better. When students have opened up to me about their hopes and fears, I have quite often found that these were similar to my own at that same age. This has given many of my students a good boost of confidence as they realise that everybody is just like them, and they don't feel so alone. As a professional, I don't get too personal on certain topics, but students—especially young children—seem to love hearing stories about adults' childhoods, how things have changed through the years, and how other things have stayed the same.

Like I've stated previously introduce a joke break time into your classroom routine to lighten the mood. The mood of the classroom is a very important factor in helping your students feel safe. Can they trust that you really care about their learning and well-being? Do they feel that their contribution to their own learning is worthwhile under your guidance? These are all questions that will float through their minds on a daily basis, and they will be watching and sensing your every move to make sure that their journey is going to be fulfilling under your educational leadership.

Experiment with different types of offbeat humour. Begin your teaching day wearing a funny or outrageous hat and pretending it's not there. Wear a pair of fairy wings and, once again, pretend they don't exist. Nothing will get your students' attention faster than doing something like this. The best part is that it will keep them on the edge of their seats waiting to see what's coming next.

The key is to just do it every now and then to add a little bit of spice to your teaching. Perhaps even decorate your classroom with streamers or party decorations for no apparent reason. Bring some bouquets of fresh flowers and place them conspicuously around your classroom. They could follow a theme or a historical event or whatever. Just make something up if you want to. Have your own classroom celebration days and get your students to even bring items in for this. The classroom is your canvas, and as the famous artist Henri Matisse once said, "Creativity takes courage."

Classroom displays are a great way to express who you are as a teacher whilst at the same time promoting a diverse range of educational mediums. This allows your students to engage in your teaching through what you believe, and if you are a great role model, they will absorb a lot of information just through what they see in their immediate classroom environment. Allow for their input by using a notice board or some wall space for their own immediate interests to be displayed. This can be a great way for them to promote themselves and how they view their world and any topic they find important enough to share with each other.

A journey of any kind begins with an idea, and then it can become a reality. Share your life journey experiences throughout your classroom. You'll be surprised at the level of interest and curiosity this can create.

Another important aspect of your classroom displays that can give off a fantastic vibe and create a theme of fun is photos. As a teacher, I have taken probably thousands photos over the years documenting my students' learning journey. Young children absolutely love seeing photos of themselves posted throughout their classroom. This also becomes a visual history of their own learning experiences. I have taken photos of every conceivable learning experience and have even just taken photos of students sitting quietly at their desks for that "natural" educational look.

This is where the fun begins. Firstly, students are always a little bit wary of a camera, as it can be a source of something that shows them in a bad light. But the more you portray them as engaging in their learning through a range of experiences, the more they will show their natural side and relax somewhat, even to the point where they won't even care that the camera is there. Once again, this is a fantastic way to build your students' self-confidence. A photo displayed in the classroom or even in a newsletter or newspaper article tells them they are appreciated and are important.

As the teacher, you can choose the mood of your classroom. Notice I didn't say *class* (as in students) but the overall feeling that goes into the physical surroundings. This is important, as the physical classroom tells students subconsciously whether they feel safe and secure in this environment. Their subconscious mind also tells them about other important aspects of you, the teacher, and whether they can trust their learning in your capable hands. Young children are very perceptive with this; toddlers even more so.

I was once asked how I measured success as a preschool teacher, since these are such complex years in a child's life when so much learning takes place. I had to think about it for a while, and then it came to me. I said,"I didn't measure the initial success by the preschoolers themselves (even though they loved being in my class) but by their younger siblings." At the beginning of every school day, the parents would stay for a little while on arrival at preschool and join in the activities, and the younger siblings would obviously be part of this too. Then the school bell would ring for the official lessons of the day to begin, and without fail, the parents would be dragging those toddlers out the door, and the toddlers would be causing a fuss about wanting to stay. This would happen on a daily basis, and as much as the parents grew weary of this scenario, they ultimately knew that their children (both the preschoolers and the siblings) were the best judges of character as to whether this was a safe and loving learning environment.

I realised that a learning environment that is safe, interesting, and above all inviting to my students is the best way to communicate that they and their learning are important to me and that as the teacher, I always want the best for them. Young children are very tuned in to who truly cares for their health, learning, and well-being and who does not. I have had the privilege of working with many inspirational teachers over the years, which has helped me with all aspects of my teaching approach. Even the teachers who at first probably didn't inspire me always gave me just that little something to take away and use for myself. I believe that everybody I have ever come into contact with in my professional circles has been there for a reason. As Wayne Dwyer states in many of his books and talks, there are no accidents or coincidences in the universe. As a teacher himself, he understood this perfectly, for himself, his teaching, and his students.

Fun can come in a lot of ways in your teaching. One of the best ways to promote it is to share your own experiences of what fun was for you as a child. I had a fantastic childhood and have always enjoyed talking about this with my students. They in turn have really appreciated and enjoyed my mini lectures about "when I was a kid" or "back in the old days when I was young." Being that a lot of my former preschool students are now teenagers and even adults, they love to hear these stories when I bump into them from time to time. They also love hearing stories about when they were preschoolers and the funny things they used to get up to.

In some teaching circles, sharing personal information is taboo—and for good reason, in many situations. You must always be aware of your professional role as teacher. But as I have mainly worked with young children, I have always enjoyed becoming good friends with many of the parents. I have also developed an uncanny ability to become good friends with many extended members, such as siblings, cousins, uncles, aunts, and grandparents. I have even been able to build many good friendships with families of students I haven't taught. This has sometimes happened by proximity, if the child was in the classroom next door or even if they are friends of the children I have taught. This networking is, I feel, a vital part of belonging to the greater community in your place of teaching and an extremely valuable part of helping your students see you once again as a people person. This shows them that you enjoy social interaction with others and that you appreciate having a variety of different people in your teaching space.

That's exactly the kind of vibe and energy I have always promoted in my classroom: the feeling that everyone is welcome and there is always something interesting and exciting going on for them to be a part of. Dan Buettner, in his book *Thrive*, describes this sense of feeling welcome in one's home or place of work as an essential part of being happy. He also suggests that as humans, we seek out interaction with others to find a sense of well-being through positive and uplifting energy with purpose.

And the best sound I have ever heard coming from a classroom, either my own or another teacher's, is the sound of children's laughter. As Jamie Blaine describes it in his insightful book *Midnight Jesus*, "Little kids' laughter is the voice of God." As a teacher and a person, I believe that with all my heart and soul.

One of the best ways to encourage laughter and a sense of fun with your students is to be the instigator of the fun. Join a school committee and help organise school dances or science fairs. Then come along dressed up as your favourite theme character or whatever. I have dressed up for many different types of extracurricular activities for a variety of events and celebrations over the years. This has earnt me a reputation for being a go-getter amongst parents and other teachers, which is great. Yet the most important reputation is the way you make your students feel when they know they are included in the fun and excitement. Be the life of the party with your students, and they will never forget it. If this is not your type of personality, develop your acting skills and play the part each teaching day.

I make this point again about how I was once told, that good teaching is not that different from good acting. You just need to know which character you will play that day and go with it. Be a little different in your teaching approach and watch and see how differently your students begin to see you. Experiment with different parts of your personality and teaching approach to keep your students guessing. This will bring a certain intrigue to your classroom, which will spark and excite their interest.

Try this with different subjects you are teaching and learn from the reactions you get. This not only can keep your own interest alive but may lead you to ideas and paths you may have never dreamed of in your teaching life. I have lived this many times in my teaching years thus far, and I hope to make this inner childlike sense of wonder last a lifetime.

Whilst I am on the subject of childlike wonder, your inner child is yet another important factor in recognising and developing your own inner child. It is that very deep part of you that will never know enough about the world you live in. Getting to know your inner child was a huge fad many years ago, with adults going back through their childhood to heal the lost or wounded child they left behind. It became a trendy psychological journey where you forgave your parents (living or deceased or even unknown) and then embarked on a journey of self-discovery. But for all its pomp and ceremony, it actually allowed us as adults to recognise and acknowledge the part of ourselves that loves to be silly or do things just for the sake of it. It meant reducing ourselves to a childlike state to really move in new directions that could have huge benefits for our adult state.

Many professions from all walks of life have seen this as a sea change where you regress to a simpler form of living just because you choose to. There were always financial constraints that had to be weighed up and lifestyles that had to be reconsidered, but the beauty of this is that one can do it anytime as a teacher. I have my own personal sea change daily with my students on a variety of topics.

For example, English becomes an investigation into the history of words and their meanings. I am forever noticing how the English language is a hodgepodge of Latin, Greek, Arabic, and many other languages thrown into a huge verbal melting pot. Being able to understand your own language means understanding yourself and how you speak. Being literate is the closest thing many of your students will ever get to having ultimate knowing of themselves and their place in the world. The ability to read, write, and think critically is the best gift any teacher could ever give them.

One of the most powerful admissions I have ever made as a teacher to my students is that I do not know everything. I even offered them the opportunity to show me things or challenge me on things I did not know. This way, they saw me as a learner just like them. I wasn't exactly a Rhodes Scholar with maths when I was at school, and I freely admit this to my students. If I get stuck on an algorithm or whatever, I am frequently consulting them in their knowledge of what it is that they know to be true. They absolutely love being called upon to assist the teacher with complex (or even basic) mathematical problems. This way, my students see me as a human and a person who yes, knows his limitations, but at the same time is willing to push beyond them with help from others.

Science was not my strongpoint in school either, but I always possessed a healthy respect and interest in all things scientific. I have always been interested in the laws of physics and how they affect us on a day-to-day basis. The laws of cause and effect are my favourites, especially how they can be incorporated into the laws of karma and spiritual attraction. I share this with my students daily, and it never ceases to amaze me how it feeds my and their interest further. Even more amazing is how this can be woven into any subject I am teaching—maths, art, geography, or whatever. These scientific laws are part of every aspect of our teaching and learning lives.

A very important aspect to having fun with your students is to let yourself look silly occasionally. Not silly in the sense of walking around with a stupid grin on your face, but rather, be a leader in taking the initiative to laugh at yourself or silly situations. Occasionally be silly just for the sake of it. Adults or grown-ups have by and large forgotten how to just be silly and to laugh at themselves.

I remember when I was growing up, my mother had attached a quote to the side of the fridge that said, "Blessed are those that can laugh at themselves for they will never cease to be amused." Our world has become too serious, with everyone walking around professing doom and gloom about the future. The world markets will crash again, an asteroid is due to hit the earth and wipe us all out, the greenhouse effect will choke us all to death or kill us all some other way. When you switch on the nightly news, you see a very sad picture. Murders, assaults, car crashes, and the like bombard our senses.

To overcome this and become an extremely positive teacher, I suggest that you develop some habits that at first may seem odd but have been around for a while and have served many educated and intelligent people well for a long time. Firstly, develop a personal filter for what it is you really want to know about something. Yes, the internet is great for researching almost anything, but it primarily contains a lot of information that for your day-to-day existence is useless. With information overload becoming a very real source of workplace stress, one needs to get into the habit of only absorbing certain amounts of information.

As a teacher, one of the greatest sources of stress is emails. Yes, they were invented as a great source of fast and efficient communication, but in recent years, I have found them to be a main source of a lot of rubbish (that is, information that is not useful to me). Everyone wants to email you something about a meeting or event or whatever, and once again, as much as this can be informative, it can also be a huge time-waster and an even huger overload on your senses. Learn to discern what is important and what is not and get into the mindset that many people do not intend to get back to you instantly with a request and you shouldn't be ready to do the same.

Phone texts are probably a preferable way to get a reply fast, but for myself I never answer or reply to anything phone-related during my teaching time. In fact, I make it a rule (and it is an actual rule in some schools) never to bring my phone into the classroom. I keep it in a staffroom or locked away in a storeroom somewhere. Yes, I do get the occasional urgent message, but I am never on call to anyone 24/7. I get back to people when it's convenient for me. If I miss something, I just apologise and move on.

Life is not about being in contact with everyone all the time. Yes, with technology, we have become a smaller world; yet that does not necessarily mean you must be part of that all the time. I'm not a technophobe, but I believe that personal space and the ability to find serenity in my life when I choose to is more important to my well-being than anything else, especially in my teaching life.

Now whilst we're talking about serenity, I would suggest getting into the habit of reading lots of books. They can be e-books if you wish or traditional paper ones, but this goes a long way to giving you power of choice over what it is you actually absorb through print. For me, I have never really been a fan of newspapers, or online news sites for that matter. It's not that I'm totally heartless or lacking compassion, but reading or hearing about all the natural or human-caused disasters in the world on daily basis does not do much for my immediate well-being.

I remember watching the Scottish comedian Billy Connelly on TV doing a skit about the news once. He said that if we all sat down and watched all the news and read every newspaper of any particular day and took every story to heart, we would be nervous wrecks within a week. Obviously, he added some funny bits in between and made fun of a few situations, but I found it very thought-provoking. I began to get into joining different world aid organisations and donating money to several causes. This gave me a sense of empowerment over the negative view of these events, as I knew I was indirectly helping others in need all over the world.

Part of having fun as you teach is to once again never forget your childish wonder. I recall the scene from the movie *Under the Tuscan Sun* in which one of the lead female characters says to another how the great Italian film director Federico Fellini once told her to never lose your childhood innocence and sense of wonder. When I first became a preschool teacher, I took the opportunity to get back in touch with my inner child. I guess it did help a lot that I was teaching four-and five-year-old children.

It still baffles me how my students, even the older ones, tend to want to grow up faster than they should. I tell them they only have a finite number of years in their childhood, but their personal childlike outlook can last forever if they wish. As much as many teachers over the years have accused me of being childish myself, I just tell them that this is what I do. I have never made excuses for wanting to be this kind of teacher, ever.

Many teachers are also wonderful at doing this, but they feel they have to disguise it as something else. It seems so sad that teachers feel they have to pretend to be something they are not or behave in certain ways because they feel silly or will lose the approval of their peers. Like the title of this chapter proudly states, just have fun.

CHAPTER 12

NEVER GIVE UP

W INSTON CHURCHILL ONCE famously said, "Never, never, never, never, never ... ever give up." He faced many extreme tests in his life and rose time and time again to become one of the greatest leaders of the twentieth century. I have found during my time as a teacher that even just saying these words of his will jar something in my mind and give me that tiny extra little bit or hope, courage, or even focus to keep going.

The reality of teaching, as with life in general, is that you will have bad days. You will even have some very bad days, and on rare occasions you will have days when teaching seems like the last profession on earth you would ever want to partake in again. But as the famous motivational speaker Les Brown put it so eloquently, "Ladies and gentlemen ... you do not have bad days ... you have character building days instead." When I first heard these words many years ago as a young teacher, this resonated with me. How you think and perceive things can be very different depending on your experiences. This also fits in beautifully with William Shakespeare's quote that "There is nothing good or bad in this world but just our thinking that makes it so." And so it has been with my teaching, and so it will be with yours.

There are a myriad of challenges and obstacles you will need to overcome in your day-to-day life as a teacher in any field. How you see them is the crucial ingredient to not only a successful outcome but also a long and happy teaching career. To not only survive in the teaching game but prosper, you will need to continually change the way you look at, act on, speak about, and feel about how you can teach your students effectively. Please do not let your mind trick you into believing that anything is "just how it is." Things can and will change, and you have to become a surfer of the highest degree to ride that wave of change.

Now I would like to tell you that yes, I have always sat right on the highest crest of that wave and rode it like a pro, but that would be untrue. I have fought change in many aspects of my teaching. At times, I have found myself unwilling to change because in my heart I knew it just didn't feel right. But I am here to tell you that some of the best lessons I have ever learnt about change within myself came the hard way.

My first and most difficult lesson came when here in Australia, they abolished play-based preschool. At the time, this was my groove, my bread-and-butter of who I was as a teacher. I have struggled with the new curriculum that has replaced it. This is still a very contentious issue for many early childhood teachers and parents, and it has led me to move in different directions as teacher. It took me out of my comfort zone and gave me new things to learn and think about. When I talk to the legendary teachers in my life, they tell me that these are exactly the kinds of things that a learning, growing, and evolving teacher needs every so often to understand that the game is constantly changing.

A big part of never giving up as a teacher is understanding and knowing yourself better. This is the key to understanding how things can work for you and how you can move forward as a teacher. Accepting certain work conditions is part and parcel of whether you will feel happy, content, and fulfilled in a situation.

Some things will become manageable, and other things won't. This can come down to the workload that you choose to take on, and yes, it is always a choice. You can come up with as many excuses as you like about why something is or isn't working for you, but ultimately you are responsible for the choices that can either alter or completely change this.

If the type of school you are teaching at doesn't suit your personal philosophy, find one that does. The same goes for teaching at a certain year level or subject. At times, you will find that you have become too comfortable with a situation. This, I recommend, is the best time to make a change.

For me, this year, like the others before it, has been crucial in allowing me a little bit of space to step back from teaching and evaluate where it is I want to go next. This choice is mine and mine alone, and I have found that when I look for new options in my teaching life, the universe always presents me with the best choice.

I'd like to say that I am always happy with this choice, but quite often have not been. What I have learnt is that the universe always puts me in the right situation for the right reasons to learn what it is exactly that I have to learn, both about myself and about my teaching. And so it can be with you. Open yourself up to the world of things you don't know, either about your teaching or yourself, and you'll be astounded by what can be presented to you.

I say *presented* because I view teaching as a gift from the heavens. I know that I was born to be a legendary teacher, but I also know, without a shadow of a doubt, that it is a blessing to be able to share the best of myself with not only my students but everybody I come into contact with. For me, the gift of being a giving person is amplified by my ability to reach into the hearts and minds of not only my students but anybody and everybody I can either educate or inspire.

Commitment is another aspect of your teaching that may inspire you to have a long and prosperous teaching career. In the present world we live in, there is at times a lack of commitment to something bigger than ourselves. Not that I'm suggesting you become a martyr and take one for the team with your teaching, but be realistic about why it is you are (or even want to be) a teacher. Really ask yourself the tough questions about whether you believe in your own mission statement for yourself in this industry.

If you are reading this and you are one of these individuals, then please consider your choice to be a teacher very carefully. Teaching does not require a high school graduation score as high as, say, medicine or law, but the long-lasting effects of teaching can make or break a child, a class, a school, or even a community. This in turn can have huge implications for how society views teaching and education as a whole.

Just after I graduated from university, I was doing a first-aid course which was a mandatory requirement for me to work as a teacher. I remember telling the first-aid instructor that I had just graduated as an early childhood teacher and needed my first-aid certificate to get a job. He laughed and asked me why I in the world I would ever want to become a glorified babysitter. This obviously shocked me, as I had to work extremely hard to obtain my degree. But I realised that this kind of back talk would only strengthen my resolve about being a legendary teacher, in a preschool or wherever.

When I became a teaching director, I told my day care centre staff at every meeting that they were not glorified babysitters but early childhood educators. This as first brought a little bit of scoffing and laughter, but as time went on, I challenged them to believe in themselves enough to see through the scorn and recognize that their job was truly important to the lives of the children we taught.

One of the most important factors in never giving up as a teacher is your self-belief. This is not only for yourself but also for the students you teach. Be a positive influence on your students and any other students you may come in contact with in your teaching job. Use positive language when teaching and interacting with your students.

The biggest mistake you can ever make as a teacher is to tell students that they will never amount to anything. This is poison both to you as a teacher and to your students. As a teacher, your main job is to build your students up and help them to see and develop their potential. You will, of course, encounter many situations where your students will not appreciate your teaching and may treat you with disrespect or distain. This will never be justification to lower yourself enough to label any student with such a ghastly title. Many times in my life, I have met people whose teachers branded them with this label, and yet despite this, they went on to have a successful life.

As a teacher and a leader, you need to always set the best example. Sure, you are only human, and on occasion you will speak your mind and let something slip that should be left to pass. But as you gain more experience, you will ultimately learn that manners are the best solution, and everyone, no matter how demanding, deserves your courtesy.

This brings me to the subject of manners in general. Manners are a big part of giving everyone you come into contact with, both as a teacher and as a person, with respect. Some people will not reciprocate, but the one thing I have always aimed to do is to be the most courteous person I can be as a teacher. In my teaching life, I've had students, parents, other teachers, and even admin staff, show me the rudest and most disrespectful behaviour ever known to the human race. Yet I am proud to say that I have never engaged in any kind of screaming or grudge match. I have even on a couple of occasions politely asked the person to keep the conversation positive and respectful, and on some occasions, they have. This has allowed me to leave the situation with a greater sense of pride in myself for not lowering my standards.

Some teachers see this as soft or weak, but I think of it as showing true inner strength. It is much more difficult to take the high road in situations where tempers can flare and emotions can get out of hand. In this way, you can demonstrate to your students (who may or may not see this) that you are always conscious of your own self-respect and your belief in yourself through your words and actions.

Teaching is like a relationship in many ways. It will bring out the best and the worst parts of your personality. Like any good relationship it will challenge you beyond your natural limits and allow you to become incredibly resilient. You will experience the highest of highs and the lowest of lows. You will laugh and cry (sometimes at the same time), but you will never be bored. The key, once again, is to never give up, and to keep coming back for one more round. Your legs will ache, your heart will pound, and every ounce of your being will be challenged beyond what's humanly possible, but never give up.

CHAPTER 13

CHANGE IS INEVITABLE

C HANGE IS A constant in the world of teaching. Perhaps the hardest part of my teaching career right now, as I write this, is coping with a lot of change in a fairly short period of time. In my twenty plus years of teaching thus far, I have witnessed five or six major overhauls of the teaching curriculum. In some ways, this is not a bad thing, as new ideas are always needed, but the way things have been going here in our education system, it's like reconditioning a truck engine after you've barely ran it in.

Every time we get a new state or federal government, they seem to think that everything about education from the last government is bad and everything they are about to introduce is revolutionary. I recall a moment many years ago when we had been through many changes and everyone had become very jaded about what the next government had in store for us as teachers. I asked a legendary teacher who was a good friend of mine what she thought of it all. She said that in her time, she had seen many changes, and she had learned that the best way to cope was to nod appreciatively, act like you are very interested, and then go back to your classroom and make it work for you any way you can.

Even now, as I write this, I compare it in my mind to our current state of affairs. In Australia, we have a national curriculum that came in a couple of years back and is still hanging around like a retired footballer who may or may not make it as a commentator. A lot of schools are following it loosely, and the odd brave (and intelligent) school has scrapped it altogether. I guess, in its defence, it did have some good points, especially the mapped-out "point and shoot" lesson sequences. But it is just another change installed by that particular government, at that particular time, with that particular education minister.

This has led me to conclude that there is no perfect curriculum or way of teaching, even as the one-size-fits-all model doesn't work for such a diverse range of schools and regions throughout our country (or any country). The combination of politics and education never ever seems to work. There is always a huge gap between what we need in this industry and what we are given—not that this is a divine revelation to anyone who has ever had any dealings with change of governments and educational policies.

Rest assured, there is hope. That hope lies inside people like you and me who want to be legendary teachers and strive for our own versions of success regardless of what the powers that be implement or modify. I strongly believe that hope comes first from individual teachers who are willing to make changes within themselves to keep things moving. The ground level is where things work best and work for the students themselves, not for politicians' egos or bureaucrats' balance sheets.

Just to keep things about teaching positive (which is the aim of this book), I recommend that you use common sense when dealing with change. There are always seasoned legendary teachers around to share your concerns with. Seek them out and listen carefully.

In researching his book *Thrive,* Dan Buettner found that the people of Mexico use humour to cope with the effects of their sometimes odd government policies. You can do this too with your teaching. I have found that without satirical humour about school life, change, and the ever present pressures on teachers, one needs to turn to humour to laugh in the face of adversity.

Legendary teachers have developed their own language to describe difficult and stressful situations. I will share some of these for the entertainment of the readers:

- A *cherub* is a badly behaved student (mainly younger children).
- An *interesting personality* is a badly behaved parent of a badly behaved student (of any age).
- *Theatrics* is bad behaviour displayed by a student (of any age), usually accompanied by a tantrum of some sort.
- A *Tantrum* is bad behaviour from a teacher, generally generated by the bad behaviour from a student (of any age).
- A *helicopter parent* is a parent obsessed with living out their own personal academic or sporting failures through their children's academic or sporting success.
- A *Black Hawk parent* is a really academically or sportingly obsessed helicopter parent who can't seem to allow their children to actually be children.
- *Cotton Wool* is the stuff that some Educational Government Departments think we should wrap our students in to keep them safe.
- *Cotton wool* is the stuff that teachers wish to stuff in their ears when listening to Educational Government Departments.
- *Hot air* is what most Educational Government Departments seem to be full of.
- *The staffroom* is a gathering place where teachers can complain about their students (and the Government).
- *The bathroom* is a gathering place where you can complain about each other (and the Government again).
- *The carpark* is a place where you can complain about your admin (and the Government once again).
- *The office* is a place where your admin can complain about you (and the Government too).
- The *powers that be* are your immediate superiors.

- The *donkey cart* is your day to day teaching load (and whether it stays balanced or not). Remember the donkey cart story.
- The *apple cart* is your school procedures and whether you wish to adhere to them (or not). Like the old expression goes, *"Don't rock the apple cart."*

You will meet many of these people and situations on your teaching journey, and the key is to keep it light. You can stand up for what you believe in, throw caution to the wind, and become a controversial teacher and lead or follow a cause. Whatever it may be, I encourage you to do it with passion.

Along those lines, I strongly suggest that you join a teachers union when you begin to teach. I know that some people have had negative experiences with unions over the years, but nothing will keep you in good stead as a teacher more than the power of a union. In this age of government cutbacks and downsizing, a union will offer you a lot more than the government ever will. I have had some fairly heated conversations around union memberships over the years, and teachers here in Australia have some of the best conditions in the developed world because of unions. I'm not into saying that everyone must be in a union—I'm just suggesting once again that you consider joining one.

CHAPTER 14

THE BALANCING ACT

$\mathbf{B}$EING A LEGENDARY teacher and being a happy, content, and fulfilled person requires a very delicate balancing act. It takes practice and dedication, and just like every other skill, it must be honed and nurtured and constantly revised. This is where play comes into play. It's the one word that as adults we seem to forget or somehow leave behind in childhood. Yet play is one of the most important factors in being a balanced and competent teacher and being able to invigorate you sense of wonder about the world you live in.

In his book *Primary Greatness*, Stephen R. Covey writes that play is the factor that can allow you be become more creative in your life. Take it away, and you abolish the creative freedom that brings with it the essence of your highest contribution. He even suggests that creative freedom can flourish when you focus on what's more important rather than what is urgent. Part of this could even be practicing the use of the word *no* in your vocabulary.

Being all things to all people in any aspect of your life can have dire consequences for your energy levels. It can put you in a frame of mind where you always aim to please others at the expense of your own priorities. Legendary teachers know the value of being firm about what they are and aren't prepared to do. It's not that they want to be insolent for the sake of it, but rather that certain tasks or responsibilities can either be handled at a later date or by someone else. Their experience tells them that some tasks require immediate action and others don't.

Getting back to the notion of play and how this can work for you as a well-balanced and legendary teacher: seek out people and interests outside of your teaching life. I have found over the years that my life became a lot more interesting and obviously enjoyable when I began to mix with as many different social groups as possible. At various points in my life, I have moved in up to ten different groups. This is not to say that you must immediately run out and become the town socialite; rather, experiment with what interests you have and where you might like to spend your time.

A well-balanced life outside of teaching could begin with a yoga class. This is great way to meet people whilst doing something healthy for your body and soul. You could take this a step further and join a gym. Gyms are a great place to work off excess stress or negative energy built up during your teaching day whilst gaining a greater sense of physical strength and stamina.

Perhaps you may wish to join a volunteer group. Get on the internet and look up some charity groups in your local area. There is always room in this world for more volunteers, and your valuable contribution to your community is always welcomed. Plus, as Dan Buettner explains in his book *Thrive*, people who volunteer on a regular basis are able to take their mind off their own problems and focus on improving someone else's life, thus creating more personal happiness.

There are many other opportunities to expand yourself and open up to a world of diversity outside of your teaching life. But be warned that this does take courage, and there may be a few personal taboos you wish to overcome before this can create a different momentum in your personal life. The biggest of these is the fear of looking silly. This unfortunately holds a lot of people back from undertaking new endeavours in their lives. Take the plunge and try something just for the sake of it. Who knows, you may actually learn something along the way.

Another aspect of being a balanced legendary teacher is learning the art of sacrifice. As a teacher, your students will know that you truly care for them when they can appreciate your personal sacrifice of giving up your time to undertake extra tasks or activities with them. Stephen Covey tells us in his book *Primary Greatness* that the art of sacrifice can create fantastic bonds with people that can only happen when one of you is willing to sacrifice personal time to others without any reward other than to help them become better people.

Obviously, as a teacher, you will be pulled between your personal and professional responsibilities like a rag doll in a tug-of-war competition. Once again, it comes down to choice and priorities. There will be family pressures, social invitations, birthdays, and sports commitments. The key is to know your limit and stick to it. Your personal health is always your highest priority, because without it, you can't function properly in any situation. Be kind to yourself and know when you need a rest from things or some time away from it all.

Teacher burnout is very real and affects many people. No teacher walking this earth is immune to it. You might think you are strong-willed and mentally tough or whatever, but the day will come when your body and your mind will say, "I need a little break from all this." Be wise and establish your personal boundaries and where your commitment lines are drawn. You can change them at any time or move them or even re-evaluate them if you wish. They are yours and yours alone. But more on this in chapter 17.

Another very important part of being a balanced teacher is to mix with people outside of your educational life who are not teachers. As teachers, we spend a lot of our waking lives together at school teaching, and as is true with any occupation, teachers will generally gravitate together in social circles also. In some cases, teachers marry other teachers because they can be sympathetic to each other's needs.

But the key to being a well-balanced teacher outside of your teaching life is to mix with as many different people as you can.

I would encourage you to find a hobby outside of teaching or join a club that doesn't necessarily attract teachers. Make a point of befriending different types of people with a range of interests. This way, you won't get caught up in teacher talk. You do enough of this in your job, and you want to limit it as much as possible in your personal life. The best part of my personal life is the fact that when people first meet me, they have no idea that I am actually a teacher. I have been complimented many times by my nonteaching friends about how I never use teacher talk outside of school. Sure, I like to debrief with my friends and relatives who are teachers from time to time, but I have learned to keep this to a bare minimum. Nothing bores people to tears or turns them off more than when teachers get together in a huddle and begin to talk shop. I try to avoid these situations if I can.

I try to have a vested interest in lots of different social circles and make a point of having friends and associates who cover a wide spectrum of the greater community. Just to add to this, as a teacher you will become friends with lots of police officers, doctors, nurses, and emergency personnel, as they form a part of the caring professions that serve our greater community.

Technology is a huge part of our lives in these modern times. But this just like anything else in teaching and learning is a delicate balancing act also. I believe that finding information in books is a lost art that students can still reap many benefits from if they know where to look. I share these thoughts with all of my students on a daily basis. Yes, using search engines on the internet is fast and convenient, but it can train students (and teachers) to become too reliant on technology. Even as I write this, I am still making handwritten notes to expand on my ideas and concepts. It's the same with journaling or keeping a diary. I personally prefer to handwrite things and use notepads and scribble ideas. I feel that I have made a conscious effort within my teaching and personal life to keep a good balance of new methods by using technology in conjunction with more traditional methods.

As a preschool teacher from way back, I can definitely see a big difference in the concentration skills and attention span of students I have taught from years past up until now. I feel that balance with technology is essential for students to make their own critical decisions about how much they will use and how much they will forego. As much as our advertising and manufacturing industries might thrive on us using the latest gadgets in the classroom, nothing beats being able to make your own decisions about how you wish to use these tools in your classroom and to what extent.

I recall when digital whiteboards first came into our teaching lives, we were told that this would revolutionise education as we knew it. As I write this, or at least in the school I am currently teaching in, I cannot think of one teacher who still uses one— perhaps mainly because they (the digital whiteboards, not the teachers) are all broken or just never seemed to work at all. No sooner had they entered our teaching lives than they needed a maintenance crew of thousands (slight exaggeration there) to keep them running properly. The screens were great to use as a wall projection tool, but then again, so were just plain old whiteboards, which you can still use in your classroom. I would hate to think about how much exactly the education departments of this great nation spent on the high-tech versions.

Just to add to this point, I am constantly amazed at how the educational system keeps telling us that technology will improve our teaching lives. I can't seem to find a teacher nowadays who can keep up with everything that technology demands. Yes, email is a great communication tool, but 90 per cent of the emails I get are completely irrelevant. Laptops are a great way to store information, yet you are constantly doing backups for your backups and wondering whether you will be able to find that missing file or is anyone hacking into your computer and spying on you (or stealing the precious book you're writing).

And as I am currently at the time of writing this book, teaching health studies with my primary (elementary) age children I have made some interesting discoveries with this. One of these being how many parents wish for their children to have less "screen time." This being where their time on laptops, ipods, ipads and phones is kept to a minimum. This in itself is also a balance and I would encourage you the teacher to also become aware of this for yourself. It is extremely easy to become addicted to your own technological devices and become consumed with all the latest fads and gadgets. I am not casting judgement on how much or little you use these but just continually urge you to become more aware of this.

CHAPTER 15

IT'S A MARATHON, NOT A SPRINT

Y our teaching journey is just what the title of this chapter says: a marathon and not a sprint. If you are a beginning teacher, you will be filled with youthful optimism (or just optimism, if you're not that youthful), and you will be eager to get into your newly chosen career and get on with it. This is obviously a great way to begin your teaching journey, but be warned that there are many pitfalls waiting for you along the way. One of the biggest is the notion of whether you as a teacher are ever doing enough.

You will see many teachers doing truckloads of extra work or taking on additional responsibilities. You will be required to do this at various points in your teaching journey as well, but beware of Martyrdom Syndrome. This is where a teacher does many extracurricular activities and loves to tell everyone about it. Take it from me: if you want to survive in the teaching game, you should get involved, but make sure that you balance your teaching and personal life. No single teacher ever holds a school or learning institution together on their solo efforts. We all want to feel that our contribution to education is important, but there is a fine line between knowing your strengths and doing things because you feel you just have to.

If you do feel pressured to do something that you either don't feel you know enough about or just don't feel comfortable with, learn to say the word *no* (once again). Now don't be like toddlers with their first word and say a blanket no to everything. There are plenty of teachers around like this too. Offer your school or learning institution a variety of options about what it is that interests you and how you can add value to your students' lives. Administrations love to hear anything that will add value to their cause.

Part of learning your limits as a teacher is to make mistakes. Mistakes will become part and parcel of your life as a teacher, especially in your early years. The more experienced you get, the more mistakes you will make, but fortunately you will know what's worth worrying about and what isn't. I read a great saying on a poster many years ago: "If you aren't making mistakes in life, then you aren't trying hard enough."

Of course, you don't want to storm off into your teaching life and be constantly falling on your face. You want to take a balanced approach to what definitely works for you and your students and what does not. This is where reflection comes in very handy.

Learn to stand back and reflect on how you see yourself as a teacher. I was once asked many years ago if I had been given my own teaching services for a year, would I be happy with the outcome? See yourself from an objective standpoint. Come at yourself from a different angle and pose new possibilities for yourself and your teaching. Learn to see each day in the big picture of being a new step towards more fantastic teaching experiences. Pace yourself with everything you do in your teaching and learn to keep things in their proper perspective.

And on the odd occasions when your energy levels run ridiculously low and you feel like you can't go on (and you will). Be kind to yourself and take the occasional day off. A tired and worn out teacher isn't going to do anyone any good.

And on the occasions when you do get sick and need time off, please use your sick leave. Don't think you are doing yourself (or your students) any favours by trying to teach when you aren't well enough to. Take care of yourself and please don't forget to also be kind to yourself.

CHAPTER 16

GO ALONG TO
GET ALONG

THIS MAY BE a controversial chapter, as it outlines my interactions with administrations I have worked with and how I have overcome the challenges these have brought. I have come to the conclusion after many years of careful reflection that the ideal way to stay in good stead with your admin is to go along with procedures and get the best out of them for yourself and for your students.

Now, I can hear lots of scoffing from experienced teachers, as they have the wisdom to know that you do not want to be a robot teacher and do everything you are instructed to, especially when you don't believe in it. But here's where it gets interesting. As a teacher, you are a professional; and as a professional, you are obligated to undertake your duties as your admin sees fit. Certainly there are power-hungry and even sadistic administrators out there in the teaching world, but all this needs to be to you is a learning experience. There is nothing good or bad about these situations providing you continually remind yourself that you are there for your students and your community at large.

You won't agree with all the decisions made by those in positions above you on the food chain, but that should never be your focus when you have a job to do. I have worked with megalomaniac admins, and I have worked with highly democratic ones too. The issue of what is right and wrong unfortunately is just a matter of perception. If you perceive something as being an act of bullying from your admin, please document your interactions and seek the correct advice or help if necessary. Talk to your teachers union about your rights and go through the correct channels if you wish to lodge a complaint. But as a teacher who has worked briefly as an admin, I have seen first-hand the unbelievable pressure they are under. Please remember that they are still human just like you. Taking the high road with any issue should always be your priority. Remember, you are all on the same team.

As a person of faith, I believe wholly in the N.I.V Bible verse "Do unto others as you would have them do unto you" (Luke 6:31). The fact of the matter is that everything you do and say to your admin you are ultimately responsible for. The admin's job is to support you and guide you, and although that may or may not be happening in certain situations, you are responsible for your words and actions. As a human being working in a giving and at times needy environment, it can be easy to forget this. Your emotions can and probably will get the best of you at times, and you will say and do things you may later regret. That being said, the one single thing I have found unbelievably helpful to me as teacher when dealing with my admin is, "Do I have all the facts about this situation? And am I making any assumptions before I act on these facts?"

I'm not going to get all high and mighty and pretend that I have done this in every situation, but the lessons I have learned from these interactions have really given me food for thought about my own perceptions on certain issues. This can work equally well when dealing with parents of students and even fellow teachers. Admins have people coming at them with a myriad of problems that need their immediate attention. Before you go running to them with your concerns about how unfair your teaching life is, please firstly ask yourself, can I solve this problem on my own? Is it a priority right now or can it wait?

If you find yourself in the unenviable position of being disciplined by your admin, take it in your stride. If you are at fault, be the first to admit it and promptly apologise. Then be sure that you do not make the same mistake twice. Admins can only extend so much forgiveness and grace to you. If there are external circumstances adding to your problem, please bring that to the admin's attention, but stay positive and keep the conversation objective. You may not know the whole story behind something, and the key to your openness is for others to bring this to your attention.

When you have the overwhelming urge to defend yourself, please just think: how important is this? It's like when as a teacher you are disciplining a student and they begin to defend their position. Nothing irritates a teacher more than students backchatting—even when they may be right. The same goes for your admin team. They may be in the wrong or may even be making a judgement call too early. Take the high road and send them (probably best in a quiet prayer) lots of love and forgiveness. Perhaps even write them a note and then hold on to it for a week and reread it. It's probably best to then destroy it, forget it, and move forwards.

As a teacher, you will learn that some battles are worth fighting and some aren't. Get in touch with who you really are and make a good judgement call for the greater good of everyone, not just yourself. If you accept a teaching job, you must accept certain situations that will come with it. Don't become a whinger or a complainer. You will inevitably come across a few of these types of people in your time. Watch how their support from admin dries up like a small puddle of water on a hot summer's day.

As Jamie Blaine explains in his classic book *Midnight Jesus*, as a psychologist and councillor he would like to "tell people to burn all their flags and embrace the illogical. To speak the truth, fight the power and truly be like history's most infamous radical, that Rebel Jesus Christ. Not if I want to keep my job though." Just like Jamie, we all have a burning desire, especially as teachers, to speak out our own version of the truth and to turn the educational world on its head with the way things should be. At times, you may even find yourself face to face with your admin team ranting and raving about injustice and freedom from oppression. But truth be known, they are feeling just like you are. They have people above them who have people above them who have an unseen entity above them who when all is said and done couldn't give two hoots what you think.

The way to true self-righteousness through your teaching is to keep doing what it is that you do in the classroom. Do what you're paid to do and leave the big issues to the powers that be, because that's why they get paid the big bucks. Add a touch of empathy to your approach to your fearless leaders, and they will actually appreciate it. Remain focused on the thought that you are once again all on the same team.

You will have differing opinions and be coming from different angles on anything and everything, but they are still the boss and you are still a teacher. As the native American proverb suggests, "Before you can judge someone, walk a mile in their shoes first." Your admins are not perfect, but be respectful of their position and give them grace and forgiveness with a smile.

CHAPTER 17

BURNOUT

B URNOUT IS A very serious issue that can make or break teachers at any time or at any stage in their teaching career. Burnout can creep up on you like the proverbial thief in the night, or it can hit you like a heavyweight boxer's punch right between the eyes. The good news is that there are lots of ways around this problem. Believe it or not, there is no problem in the world that another teacher just like you hasn't stared down and overcome.

The essence of burnout stems from the fact that you take on too many tasks within your teaching load. As a new teacher, this can be very easy to do, as there really isn't anyone to tell you to stop. In fact, if you are eager and willing, you quite often don't have any problems with suddenly having too much on your plate. But burnout can be easily fixed if you admit to yourself that perhaps a situation isn't working for you and you need to change it.

A bigger part of teacher burnout is not having enough outlets in your life away from teaching. Yes, teaching is a great profession that I obviously love, but it is a job that can totally consume you, especially if you don't get your work–life balance happening properly.

Another aspect to overcoming or avoiding burnout is managing stress. In teaching, there is good stress, which doesn't necessarily bother you when you're in the zone, and bad stress, which can make your life unbearable. Know your triggers—the things that put you into a less-than-ideal frame of mind. They can be lack of sleep, not eating properly, not preparing your lessons properly, and so on. I have, like all teachers, suffered under stressful conditions, some my own doing and others not. But at the end of the day, you have to know how much teaching work you are prepared to do and when to stop and take a break till tomorrow.

Dr. Dina Gloubermann, in her book *The Joy of Burnout*, describes in great detail how burnout should be embraced and celebrated as a step in a new direction. She offers an insightful perspective from her own experiences with burnout and how this can be a sign that something within your belief system needs to take a new course. Quite often this has been the case for me, and when I have been forced into changing course in my teaching life, it's always turned out for the best and brought me many new fantastic experiences. When I look back on the times in my teaching life when I was feeling burnt out, I always remember it as being the birth of a new mindset that was either ready to be adopted or badly overdue. In many ways, it has to be done, and you know full well that the way you are currently operating as a teacher isn't working and a change is actually needed.

I have found out that burnout never seems so bad in hindsight; in many ways, it has almost seemed somewhat silly. I often think back and wonder why in the world was I hanging on so tightly to a perception that was either outdated or just not working. Perhaps this also comes down to a lack of experience in a particular part of my teaching that I later learnt and corrected along the way. I'm not advocating that you actively seek to burn yourself out, just to know where your limits are and keep it somewhere in the back of your mind that workaholic teachers are not necessarily effective teachers.

The most difficult part of teaching in any capacity today is that there seems to be more pressure placed on teachers to perform better. Governments every so often want to score political points by having a dig at teachers and accusing us of being lazy. One thing that I have never agreed with is that teachers should do more as part of their job description. If they want to do more and can see true value in this, I am all for it, but it must be giving willingly rather than under duress.

As you become more senior in your teaching years, your responsibilities will increase along with your pay. But understand that the best way to be a legendary experienced teacher is to find the extracurricular activities that actually suit your interests and lifestyle. This can then become a win–win–win for you, your school or college, and ultimately your students.

To be realistic, you will get stuck with something somewhere in your teaching life that doesn't appeal to you one little bit. This is where your mindset comes into play. Think about how you can make it fun and learn something along the way. I once did this with a non-religion class I had a year or two back. This is a class for all students who don't follow a particular religion at school. Therefore they are all sent to one designated classroom to follow the teacher's instructions. As there was no set lesson, the students were just asked to find something to do. For fourth-graders, this meant getting bored and causing trouble. In an attempt to make this transitory lesson more palatable, I asked them what they would rather be doing. The reply was "having fun." This led me to rack my brains about how to captivate their attention for that thirty minutes each week. Then it came to me: teach them some thinking games.

I began to teach them how to play such games as noughts and crosses (tic-tac-toe) and S.O.S. As these are both sitting games where you play against each other, we had a competition of sorts develop. As the teacher and role model, I would gladly allow the students to challenge me to a game. One game of S.O.S between myself and one of the students lasted for four straight weeks. This not only taught these students how to play games and follow rules but also how to occupy themselves with strategies and moves they could share with each other week to week.

Burnout can unlock potential within yourself if you let it. The one aspect of myself that I am constantly amazed by is my ability as a teacher to keep pulling ideas and energy out of thin air. When I look back at times of stress and feel that sense of hopelessness, a better solution always seems to come by itself. This is where faith comes into play. Even as a spiritual teacher (or a teacher of spiritual inclinations), I'm not talking about a faith in something greater than yourself—even though that still helps—but mainly a faith in yourself. Self-belief can and will carry you to new heights beyond what you can already see.

If other factors are present in your life, such relationship problems, health problems, and the like, these can compound your stress levels for sure. The best solution I have found is to focus on one task at a time and do it until it's done. Don't skim and try to do twenty things at once. At times just admitting to your co-workers and superiors that things aren't working out can be a godsent. They have all been there too and can arrange help on many different levels if you need it. Don't ever get into the habit of thinking that you are alone and that everybody else has it all together. The teachers I have met who claim to have it all together all the time are only kidding themselves.

There will be times in your teaching when you have the Midas touch and other times when your teaching resembles a dog's dinner. But that, believe it or not, is the best part about continuing your own personal journey of self-discovery and self-renewal. Finding new directions within your teaching journey is the key to a successful teaching life.

You will meet the odd teacher who has been working at the same school forever. Not to say that this is a bad thing, but the real essence of legendary teachers is that they are not afraid to admit they don't know something and move to new teaching places and spaces to gain a new perspective and undertake or hone new skills. I sincerely believe that in a lot of ways, being stressed about some aspect of your teaching or even being on the verge of burnout is your soul's way of saying that a change is needed and you must become aware of how to create more options in your teaching life to make worthwhile changes for the better.

When I think back to the most stressful times in my teaching life and give thanks for getting through it, I look back now and have a sense of how strong I became when I really needed to. This surprises me somewhat; even though I love being a teacher and would like to think that I am extremely dedicated to my students, I am still amazed by the inner strength that seems to always carry me through. This has partially to do with self-love and self-belief but also with the realisation that nothing in any aspect of my life ever stays the same or lasts forever. Once I realised that change will be a constant part of my life, things seemed to fall into place.

When I get down about something, I sometimes tell myself how bad things are, but at some point I realise that this is only an event or a particular situation that needs to be dealt with and discarded. This may sound simplistic, but it just comes down to making a decision for myself to keep moving forward and not stagnate or dwell on something for too long. A great way to keep moving forward, for me, is to use positive affirmations each and every day. I once shared these with a fellow teacher who didn't believe in them and asked me why I had to be so positive about everything. My instant reply was that being positive was the only way for me to be open to finding a solution to problems, and besides that, being negative doesn't do anyone any good in any situation.

In his book *Calm at Work*, Paul Wilson describes workplace stress as not being about time responsibilities or pressures but what's going on inside your head—how you are or are not prioritising or organising things. When you prepare yourself properly for tasks and set a personal rhythm for getting things done, you find your sweet spot or groove. Even though you may be busy with all your teaching commitments, they are still getting done and you are moving through your teaching day with a feeling of accomplishment. The important thing to remember here is that this will give you a greater feeling of control over changes and when and how they should occur in your teaching life. Some of these changes can even be experimental on your part. You could work at developing a mindset that requires you to acknowledge that there are no mistakes in your teaching life, only learning experiences and opportunities for growth and expansion.

Accordingly to Dan Buettner in his book *Thrive*, happiness and contentment at work are not products of dedication and hard work. Rather, as he discovered in Denmark, where citizens keep their work–life balance in check, it's more about understanding that one needs to keep interesting and fun things in one's life. Isolation—either by becoming a workaholic or shutting other aspects of interest out of your life—does nothing for your well-being or livelihood In the long term. Understanding that the world will still turn whether your work harder or not is a good enough reason to keep your mind focused, but also be open to anything that may or may not be productive for you or your students.

CHAPTER 18
BELIEVE IN YOURSELF

I F YOU ONLY remember one thing from this book, it is the ability to believe in yourself. This may again sound like some kind of emotional pep up but this is the one factor that will make or break you as a teacher and more importantly as a person. And always keep in mind that to be given a job as a teacher is an extreme privilege and not a right. Sure, you may have or be working towards the qualifications and experience to do the job, but it's the ability to stay humble and grateful in your role that determines how your teaching life is governed. And as you've read here and perhaps already discovered for yourself, is that teaching in my opinion is one the most highly esteemed jobs in our community.

When I tell new people that I meet that I am a teacher and I say it with true pride and conviction, they tend to give me a higher degree of respect. This is often followed by the comment of "How do you do it." To which I promptly reply, "I do it very well thank you, because it's what I love to do." And I urge you as a teacher or prospective teacher to take this approach also.

Avoid stating things like, "I'm just a teacher", as this can make you sound average. And there is nothing average about you as a teacher or anybody who willingly chooses to stand in front of a classroom full of learners and inspire them to become the best version of themselves that they can be. Be proud of yourself and most importantly be proud of your profession.

And add just once again some spiritual faith to yourself to give you that magic touch. When you are able to hand over the load from your teaching day to a power greater than yourself you will see the flow of your teaching journey unveil itself.

I will finish this book with another short story about how I learnt the value of letting go and letting things flow in my teaching.

A year or so back I was charged with organising a school dance (disco). I recall setting aside a large portion of time to allow all the key ingredients for this event to be a huge success.

Firstly I picked a theme that I liked, which was the 1970's. I knew my students would also love it as I had spent many years indoctrinating them on the legendary music from that era. I set about planning the food, the advertising, the D.J, the lights, my Elvis Las Vegas costume, some photo displays, some slideshows, some friends to bring their 1970's cars along to display and a few other things also.

Yes, it was going to be bigger than Ben-Hur with a cast of thousands. About a week or so before the event a lot of these things either weren't happening or were just out there but not quite ready.

I questioned my belief (and my organisational skills) about whether things were all going to happen the way I had imagined. I recall sitting down in my favourite meditation chair in my living room and going through all the things that had to be checked off during that following week. I mentally identified the 7 major factors that would make or break this event and were by my own perceptions critical to everything being a success. I began to breathe, then closed my eyes and mentally examined every one of these 7 aspects one by one. I assured myself that firstly I had done everything possible to make them happen. And then secondly, I assured myself that they would be happening in the way they were meant to happen. Then I let them all go to the divine powers that were beyond my control.

This was a true test of my faith both in my ability to truly let go and to truly believe that the divine powers would deliver everything as requested. And just like magic with each passing day leading up to the event, it all fell exactly into place. The evening was nothing short of an extravaganza on an epic scale. It was a night that everybody talked about for a long, long time (almost went down in our school history books). Everyone was amazed at how everything just came together when it needed to. I also learnt from this that sometimes in my teaching life I just needed to get out of my own way and let the flow do what it's going to do. And things always just have a way of working themselves out.

With that I would still like to encourage you to be the best version of your teaching and learning self that you can be also. And may the teaching Gods bless you always.

I will leave you with a quote that I have on the side of a coffee cup that I presently have on my teaching desk at school (which I actually keep pencils in, not coffee).

"A hundred years from now, it will not matter what my bank account was, the sort of house I lived in or the kind of car I drove. But the world may be different because I was important in the life of a child."

BIBLIOGRAPHY

Baker, K., ed. *New International Version Study Bible*. Grand Rapids, MI: Zondervan Publishing House, 1995.

Blaine, Jamie. *Midnight Jesus: Where Struggle, Faith, and Grace Collide*. Nashville: W Publishing Group, 2015.

Bernstein, Gabrielle. *The Universe has your back: Transform fear to faith*. U.S.A: Hay House, 2016.

Brett, Regina. *God is Always Hiring: 50 Lesson for Finding Fulfilling Work*. New York: Hachette Book Group, 2015.

Buettner, Dan. *Thrive: Finding Happiness the Blue Zones Way*. Washington, DC: National Geographic Society, 2010.

Canfield, J. & Hansen, M.V. *Chicken Soup for the Soul*. U.S.A: Health Communications Publishing, 1993.

Carnegie, Dale. *How to stop worrying and start living*. U.K: Random House, 1984.

Carnegie, Dale. *How to Win friends and Influence People*. U.S.A: Simon and Schuster, 1936

Chapman, Gary. *The 5 Love Languages: The Secret to Love That Lasts*. Chicago: Northfield Publishing, 2015.

Charles, C.M. *Building classroom discipline*. New York: Longman. 1999.

Covey, Stephen R. *Primary Greatness: The Twelve Levers of Success*. New York: Simon and Schuster, 2015.

Covey, Stephen R. *The Third Alternative: Solving Life's Most Difficult Problems*. New York: Simon and Schuster, 2011.

Dyer, Wayne W. *Excuses Begone..* U.S.A: Hay House, 2009.

Dyer, Wayne W. *Inspiration: Your ultimate calling.* U.S.A: Hay House, 2006.

Dyer, Wayne W. *Your Erroneous Zones.* U.S.A: Harper-Collins, 1976.

Gazda, George M, et.al. *Human Relations Development: A Manual for Educators.* Boston: Allyn and Bacon, 1999.

Gloubermann, Dina. *The Joy of Burnout.* London: Hodder and Stoughton, 2003.

Keating, Kathleen. *The Little Book of Hugs.* Australia:Angus and Robertson Publishers, 1983.

McGonigal, Kelly. *The Willpower Instinct: How Self-Control Works, Why It Matters and What Can You Do To Get More Of It.* New York: Penguin Group, 2012.

Robbins, A. *Unlimited Power.* London: Simon and Schuster, 1986.

Robbins, A. *Awaken the Giant Within.* New York: Simon and Schuster, 1991.

Vinton, Elizabeth C. *How to Set Limits: Defining Appropriate boundaries of Behaviour for your Children-from Infants to Teens.* Chicago: Contemporary Books, 1998.

Wilson, P. *Calm at Work.* Australia: Penguin Books, 1997.

Zukav, Gary. *The Dancing Wu Li Masters.* New York: Harper-Collins, 1979.

Zukav, Gary. *The Heart of the Soul: Emotional Awareness.* New York: Simon and Schuster, 2001.

Printed in the United States
By Bookmasters